Essential Histories

Campaigns of the
Norman Conquest

Essential Histories

Campaigns of the
Norman Conquest

Matthew Bennett

First published in Great Britain in 2001 by Osprey Publishing,
Midland House, West Way, Botley, Oxford OX2 0PH, UK
443 Park Avenue South, New York, NY 10016, USA

ISBN 978 1 84176 228 9
Editor: Rebecca Cullen
Design: Ken Vail Graphic Design, Cambridge, UK
Cartography by The Map Studio
Index by Michael Forder
Picture research by Image Select International
Origination by PPS Grasmere Ltd., Leeds, UK
Printed and bound in China by L. Rex Printing Company Ltd

07 08 09 10 11   11 10 9 8 7 6 5 4 3 2

For a complete list of titles available from Osprey Publishing
please contact:

NORTH AMERICA
Osprey Direct, C/o Random House Distribution Center,
400 Hahn Road, Westminster, MD 21157
E-mail: info@ospreydirect.com

ALL OTHER REGIONS
Osprey Direct UK, P.O. Box 140, Wellingborough, Northants,
NN8 2FA, UK
E-mail: info@ospreydirect.co.uk

www.ospreypublishing.com

Contents

Introduction

As dusk fell on 14 October 1066, Harold Godwineson, king of England, lay dead. He had fought a day-long battle against foreign invaders but had been wounded in the eye by an arrow, knocked over in a mounted charge, and hacked to death by the horsemen's swords whilst defenceless on the ground. The result of the battle of Hastings is usually seen as 'The Norman Conquest'. There is more to war than battles though, and William, duke of Normandy, had many long years of campaigning ahead of him before he could be certain of keeping the crown that he received on Christmas Day 1066. The long-lasting impact of the invasion was a new, largely French-speaking, ruling elite accompanied by sweeping reforms in the practice and personnel of the Church, and closer economic, political and strategic ties with the Continent now that the king was also a French prince. This was

Invasion! The Norman fleet sails for Pevensey overnight (27/28 September 1066). The ship depicted is Duke William's, with a lantern at her masthead and the golden figure of a boy blowing a trumpet. This is just as she is described in written sources, named the *Mora*. Although called a tapestry, the source is a 70m-long (230ft) embroidery created within a decade of the events shown. Odo, bishop of Bayeux, had it made and possibly first displayed at the consecration of his new cathedral in 1077. (Bayeux Tapestry. With special permission of the town of Bayeux)

to affect the development of England for the next century and a half (after which Normandy was lost to the French Crown), and through the entire medieval period. Henry V's reconquest of Normandy in the early fifteenth century lasted a generation, Henry VIII's campaigns revived the policy, and English monarchs retained a claim to the kingdom of France until 1801.

There was a moment during the battle of Hastings when the cry went up that William had been killed, which was only scotched by him galloping through his ranks with his helmet pushed back to show his face to his frightened men. Everything might have changed if he had taken a dangerous wound; all would certainly have been different if he had been less of a man than he proved himself to be in the years following 1066. When rebellion broke out against his rule late in 1067 he was abroad in his duchy, but he sailed across the Channel in November – usually considered an impossible time to make the crossing – and conducted a campaign deep into the south-west during the coldest months of the year. Three times in the succeeding years he marched north to combat rebellion and invasion at York. Everywhere he went he planted castles and left garrisons under trusted *vassals* to enforce his rule. He was ruthless in pursuing the most determined resistance to its end, laying waste the northern counties and crossing the Pennines in the mid-winter of 1069/70. He plunged deep into *the Fens* with men on land and in ships, bringing siege engines to Ely abbey against the last rebel, Hereward, in 1071. In 1072 he marched to Scotland, again accompanied by a fleet, to win submission from the King of Scots.

These wars secured William's kingdom, supported by administrative reforms and the creation of records of government, epitomised by Domesday Book. This remarkable survey was the product of a warrior king's need for money. Just two years before he died, William feared invasion from Denmark, and raised a huge force of paid soldiers and sailors to oppose it. The cost was so overwhelming that, during his Christmas court at Gloucester that year, the king demanded to know how much England could produce in tax revenue to pay for the defence of his realm. The action was typical of the man, of his obsessions and of his need to be in control. The result was a remarkable document which provides insights into English society of a thousand years ago that are unmatched elsewhere.

The Norman Conquest is not viewed by everyone in today's Britain as a welcome event, and its results are still much disputed, but its history was of successful military campaigns conducted by a remarkable warrior who has left his mark on much of our history. Nor did William achieve his goals single-handedly. He proved an adroit leader of men with the ability to create a loyal following that combined hard-bitten warriors and clever clerics. He proved himself capable of operating on all fronts: personally as a soldier and inspiring leader, and, less directly, through the agency of others with specialist skills in diplomacy, administration, law and Church reform. All these attributes combined to make the events in 1066–1072 not just an invasion but a conquest and a transformation of English society.

Chronology

Northern campaign:
20 September Tostig and Harald
Hardrada defeat the northern earls
Edwine and Morkere at Fulford Gate;
King Harold marches north
25 September Harold surprises
and defeats the invaders and kills
their leaders at the battle of
Stamford Bridge
Southern campaign:
28 September William's fleet sails
into Pevensey Bay
1 October Harold marches south;
reaches London **6 October** to
gather forces
13 October Harold's army musters at
Caldebec Hill
14 October William defeats and kills
Harold and his two brothers
15–20 October Victorious army rests
at Hastings
21 October Advance to Romney,
resistance punished leading to the
surrender of Dover; outbreak of
dysentery (**21–28 October**)
November William advances to
London but finding the fortified
bridge defended against him, burns
Southwark and moves upriver
November Reinforcements land
at Southampton; Winchester
submits; William receives submission
of Archbishop Stigand when
crossing the Thames at Wallingford;
he then swings north of London
mid-December Edgar aetheling
and English leaders submit at
Berkhamsted
25 December William crowned by
Ealdred, archbishop of York, at
Westminster
1067   **Easter** William returns to
Normandy leaving his brother Odo
and William fitzOsborn in charge of
the kingdom;
Eadric the Wild raids Hereford
Autumn Eustace of Boulogne
attempts to seize Dover but
is driven off; William returns in
November

1068   Exeter rises in rebellion
January–February William besieges
the town; his army takes heavy losses
before it submits. Campaigns in
Devon and Cornwall, suppressing
the uprising
Summer William conducts his first
northern campaign via Warwick,
Nottingham, York; returns via
Lincoln, Huntingdon, Cambridge,
constructing castles at all these places
1069   **January** Robert de Commines, earl of
Northumbria, and his men massacred
at Durham; York besieged by forces
of Edgar
February–March William marches
north, surprises the rebels and defeats
them; builds second castle in York;
returns to Winchester by Easter
August Danish fleet attacks Kent then
sails north to the Humber; supports
Edgar in attacking York. One castle
falls and William Malet holds out in
the other. Other risings in Devon and
Cornwall, Shropshire, Staffordshire
and Cheshire (Eadric the Wild
and Welsh)
September William advances
from Gloucester to York. Danes
avoid battle
Christmas William holds his court
at York
1070   **January** William advances to the
Tees; Harrying of the North –
'scorched earth' tactics. William
advances across the Pennines in
mid-winter, despite a mutiny;
surprises Chester rebels. Returns to
Winchester for Easter
May Swein of Denmark joins his
fleet and sails to Ely to support
Hereward's rebellion
1071   Edwine rebels but is killed by his own
men; Morkere joins rebels at Ely
Summer William attacks Ely by land
and with his fleet; rebels surrender
1072   William leads forces north to Scotland
by land and sea. Malcolm, King of
Scots, submits at Abernethy,
confirming the Conquest

The North Sea countries c. 1066

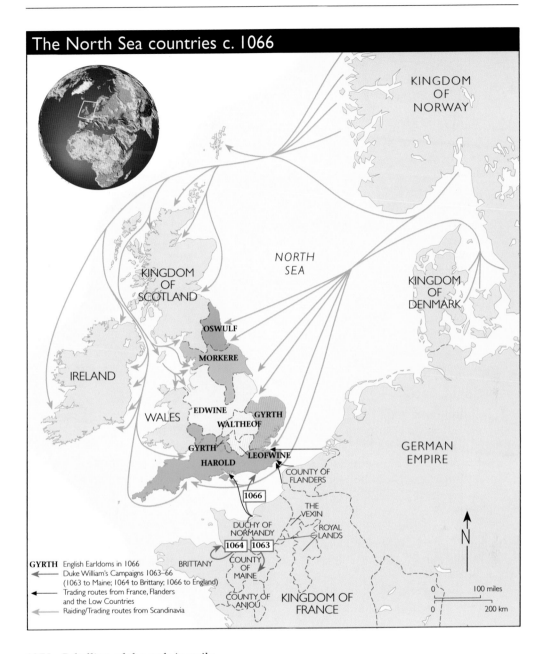

GYRTH   English Earldoms in 1066
⟵   Duke William's Campaigns 1063–66
          (1063 to Maine; 1064 to Brittany; 1066 to England)
⟵   Trading routes from France, Flanders
          and the Low Countries
⟵   Raiding/Trading routes from Scandinavia

1075 Rebellion of the earls is easily
          defeated
1079 Robert Curthose rebels against
          his father; King Malcolm ravages
          the north
1080 Robert, now reconciled, leads an army
          against Scotland
1085 Threat of Danish invasion
1086 Survey of England and the creation of
          Domesday Book
1087 Death of William the Conqueror

Danes, Normans and the English royal succession

The eleventh century in England could easily be described as the 'Scandinavian Era'. It began with a renewal of the viking raids that had plagued the reign of King Alfred (871–899). What made him 'Great' was his ability to completely reform the military and naval forces of his own realm, Wessex, and to transform them into a machine for conquest which created the kingdom of England. In addition to men and ships Alfred developed a system of fortifications, called *burhs* (boroughs). This enabled him to defend his own territories, and allowed his successors to expand into the *Danelaw*, as the territory north and east of Watling Street (the modern A5), which had fallen under Scandinavian domination, was known. The last independent viking ruler, Erik Bloodaxe, 'king' of York, was killed in 955, heralding almost half a century of peace in England.

The very wealth and success of the kingdom under Edgar (959–975) and Aethelred II (who came to the throne in 978 after his brother died in suspicious circumstances) made England a viable target for raiders. In about 991, a group of vikings defeated ealdorman Byrthnoth and the *fyrd* (army) of East Anglia at Maldon in Essex. They were paid a tribute of '£10,000' to persuade them to go away. This they did not do, however, and the following year dispersed an English fleet sent against them. In 993/94 Olaf Tryggvason launched an attack on the port of London. Olaf was bought off for a further sum of £16,000, although he did accept Christianity and returned to Scandinavia. He may already have been accompanied by Swein Forkbeard, king of Denmark, and it was the Danes who proved to be greatest threat over the next decade.

The Norman connection

In 1002, Aethelred married Emma, daughter of Richard, duke of Normandy, so forging an alliance with a ruler who had been giving shelter to viking fleets. In the same year, Swein received '£24,000' tribute.

An Anglo-Danish *huscarl*. The title means 'household warrior', who provided the core of pre-Conquest English armies. Every great lord had such a following, equipped with sword, axe or spear and protected by a mail coat to enable them to fight in the front rank in battle. He carries a kite-shaped shield which was replacing the old-fashioned round type in the 1050s. (Paul Hitchen)

Aethelred has been much criticised for paying this *Danegeld*, since the attacks continued; but it was a policy which even Alfred had used, literally buying time in order to reorganise his forces. In 1008, Aethelred tapped the considerable wealth of his kingdom to have 200 ships built and coats of armour and helmets made to equip 9,000 men. In 1012, he took into his service one of the most prominent vikings, Thorkell the Tall, whose aid proved vital in the defence of London, in return for a payment known as the *heregeld* (army tax). In the end, none of this effort prevailed against Swein, who effectively conquered the kingdom between 1010 and 1013, forcing Aethelred to send his family into exile with his in-laws in Normandy. On Swein's death in February 1014, he was succeeded by his son Cnut. Aethelred did return to contest the throne but died in April 1016, leaving his eldest (illegitimate) son Edmund 'Ironside' to continue the war. Despite putting up a brave fight, Edmund was eventually mortally wounded, leaving Cnut the undisputed ruler of England, who took Emma as his queen.

Meanwhile, in Normandy, Emma's kinsmen sheltered two young princes: Alfred and Edward. In 1035, Cnut died leaving a disputed succession, and both of them seem to have attempted a military coup. Edward landed at Southampton but was driven off, while Alfred disembarked at Dover, apparently seeking to meet his widowed mother at Winchester. On the way he fell in with one of Cnut's most prominent *earls*, a man named Godwine, who promptly handed him over to the new king, Harold, an illegitimate son of Cnut. Alfred did not long survive, and died soon afterwards having been blinded and sent to the monastery at Ely. Harold still had a rival though: Harthacnut, the legitimate son of Cnut and Queen Emma, who succeeded Harold on his death in 1040. The following year, Harthacnut invited his half-brother Edward to return to the kingdom he had fled as a child 25 years earlier, as his heir presumptive. In 1042, Harthacnut died, apparently after a heavy bout of drinking, and the old English line was restored.

The rise of Godwine and his sons

King Edward brought with him a lot of continental baggage. He had been raised in a French-speaking court, had a debt of gratitude to his Norman kin and many contacts with northern French ecclesiastics. One man he did not favour was Godwine, whom he deemed responsible for his brother Alfred's death. Yet Godwine, as earl of Wessex, was too powerful to oppose – so the new king found himself married to Edith, Godwine's daughter, in 1045. In the same year Edward installed Robert, abbot of Jumièges (a prominent Norman monastery near Rouen), as bishop of London, and a political ally. In 1048, Robert was elevated further to be archbishop of Canterbury, much to the disgust of the English Church establishment. Yet most of England south of a line drawn between the Bristol Channel and the Wash was in the hands of Godwine and his offspring, the Godwinesons. The eldest, Swein, who held a swathe of territory from Buckinghamshire into the West Country and the Welsh border, proved himself a violent maverick. After abducting and raping an abbess (for which he did penance), he went too far in 1050, by murdering his cousin Beorn, and fled to Flanders. Edward's dislike of his wife's family surfaced dramatically in 1051.

In September that year, another brother-in-law, Eustace of Boulogne (married to Edward's sister Goda), landed at Dover. In an incident which may have been no more than a dispute over lodgings (but which could have had more sinister implications), fighting broke out between Eustace's followers and the Dover townsmen. Several were killed on each side, with each blaming the other for starting it. Eustace then went to the king, who was in his favourite hunting lodge near Gloucester, and demanded recompense. Edward ordered Godwine, as earl of Kent, to *harry* the town (a common punishment for disobedience involving the destruction of buildings and property), but Godwine refused. Instead, he rallied Swein and his second son Harold, earl of East Anglia, to his cause. Raising troops, they advanced upon Edward at Langtree, in Gloucestershire, and counter-demanded that Eustace be handed over to them.

Although Edward was in a weak position, he was not helpless. This evident act of treason enabled him to call upon the support of his other earls, Leofric of Mercia (whose earldom comprised the northern midland *shires*) and Siward, earl of Northumbria. Both sides then agreed that it would be foolish to fight, as this would weaken the kingdom in the face of its enemies, and instead arranged to meet in London on 24 October to reach a legal judgement on the case. Before this

meeting could come about, however, Godwine and his sons found that their retainers began to desert them rather than face royal justice. Taking ship from Bosham, on the Sussex coast, the family fled abroad, Godwine and Swein to Flanders, to the court of Count Baldwin, and Harold to Ireland. Edward's victory seemed complete. The king re-distributed the earldoms: the south-western shires went to Odda; a strip of territory from Hereford to Oxford to Edward's nephew, Ralph; East Anglia to Aelfgar, son of Leofric of Mercia; whilst Edward retained control of the rest of Wessex. At the same

time he dealt with another source of dispute at court by installing his chaplain, Thomas, as bishop of London, in the place of an English prelate, Sparrowhawk. However, loyalties to the Godwine clan were not so easily broken as might at first appear.

Over the winter, Godwine's agents were busy on the south coast and in the eastern shires, winning the support of the men who provided naval service in the area. In the spring Godwine set out with a few ships to land in Kent, but the fleet lying at Sandwich deterred him so he sailed to the Isle of Wight, where he met Harold coming with

nine ships from Ireland. They then returned to Sandwich, raising naval forces as they advanced, until they could threaten London itself. They advanced upon the city, their ships keeping to the south bank, passed the bridge (which suggests some collusion since it withstood determined viking attacks in 1012), and joined up with land forces which had also mustered to their aid. Once again, fighting was avoided, but only at the cost to Edward of total capitulation to Godwine's demands. The dispute was blamed on the 'Frenchmen' whom the king had assembled round him, and most were expelled, including Robert, archbishop of Canterbury, and Thomas, bishop of London. The exiling of these prominent ecclesiastics was to have serious implications for King Harold's cause 24 years later.

That King Edward had not given up on finding an alternative to a Godwineson heir was made apparent in 1057. In that year there arrived in the country his cousin, a son of Edmund Ironside, called Edward the Exile. This title referred to his sojourn in Hungary to escape the attentions of King Cnut, just as King Edward had spent time in Normandy. The Anglo-Saxon Chronicle is less than explicit about the new arrival's fate, merely commenting: 'We do not know for what reason it was brought about that he was not allowed to see [the face] of his kinsman ...', which may imply that the author suspected foul play. Edward the Exile's mysterious demise did not entirely end the prospects for Aethelred's line, for he left an infant son, Edgar. Known as the *aetheling* (prince), and only a teenager, he was to play a significant role in the events of 1066 and the campaigns of the Conquest.

A group of mounted warriors practise the tactic of the close-order charge with lances couched. Holding the weapon tightly under the arm united man and horse into a single projectile. This enabled the rider to unhorse an opponent in the cavalry skirmishes that made up much of the warfare of northern France. These warriors were called *chevaliers*, but in England became known as knights. From left to right are two figures wearing mail armour, then scale and lamellar, both constructed from small metal plates sown onto a leather backing. (Christa Hook)

Harold and William: the war lords

Harold Godwineson's military reputation

At Easter 1053, Godwine seems to have had a stroke while at the king's table. His demise led to another shuffling of the earldoms, in which Harold gave up East Anglia to Aelfgar in return for Wessex, while also gaining the lands of Swein (who had died returning from a propitiatory pilgrimage to Jerusalem). He was the most powerful man in the land. The kingdom needed an effective military leader, though, because of the threat from the Welsh. This came mainly from the aggression of Gruffudd ap Llywelyn (Griffith), who had made himself king over most of Wales. In 1055, when Aelfgar found himself charged with treason and forced into exile, he fled to Ireland and attempted to reinstate himself with Griffith's help. Together they attacked Herefordshire and inflicted a serious defeat

Harold Godwineson, earl of Wessex, as *dux Anglorum* (commander-in-chief of the English). He is represented as a powerful lord with his military following and all the trappings of wealth: fine horses, hounds and a hunting bird at his wrist. He is setting off on an embassy to Normandy from his port at Bosham, on the West Sussex coast, near Chichester. (Bayeux Tapestry. With special permission of the town of Bayeux)

upon its earl, Ralph 'the Timid'. In the following year, Griffith defeated and killed the martial bishop of Hereford. In 1057, Aelfgar succeeded his father as earl of Mercia, only to find himself once more exiled and reinstated with Griffith's aid. Aelfgar died in 1062, leaving his earldom to his young son Edwine. Harold then exacted a terrible revenge. In conjunction with his younger brother Tostig, who had been made earl of Northumbria in 1055, he launched a brilliant campaign against the, by now, ageing Welsh king. In the autumn of 1063 and early 1064, a two-pronged attack by land and sea drove Griffith into flight. Despairing, his own retainers cut off his head and sent it to Harold, as mark of their surrender. The impact of Harold's attack was so great that, even at the end of the twelfth century, the Welsh-born historian Gerald of Barry could write with approval of his military genius. As far as contemporaries were concerned Harold had justified himself to be *subregulus* (under-king) and *dux Anglorum* (commander-in-chief of the English). Yet, although he was not to know it, Harold was soon to meet his rival for the English throne and eventual conqueror.

William the Bastard, duke of Normandy

William had been born in 1027/28, the illegitimate son of Duke Robert (1028–1035) and Herlève (usually called a 'tanner's daughter' but actually her father was both a rich Rouen merchant and court chamberlain). In 1033, his father decided to go on a pilgrimage to Jerusalem (quite possibly because he wished to be forgiven for poisoning his brother to gain the duchy), from which he never returned. Before he left, Robert made all his barons swear an oath that they would be loyal to his young son, and appointed guardians and a tutor for his upbringing. All went well until William's military guardian, Gilbert of Brionne, was murdered in an internecine conflict in 1040. From then on, order broke down in the duchy as individual barons tried to enlarge their own territories and constructed castles to defend them. William was helpless: his steward Osbern was killed before his eyes one night, and had it not been for the support of his uncle Mauger, archbishop of Rouen, and his step-family (his mother had married Herluin de Conteville soon after Robert's death), he

Duke William is shown discussing preparations for invasion of England. He is in discussion with half-brother Odo, bishop of Bayeux. To the right of the picture a carpenter, carrying an adze, prepares to work on the new ships required. (Bayeux Tapestry. With special permission of the town of Bayeux)

might not have survived. But survive he did, and saw his first battle at Val-ès-Dunes, at the age of 18, in the army of Henry, king of France, who came to put down a rebellion against the young duke in western Normandy (1047).

William's military education

William's training in the art of war was a hard one. He gained experience in the raids and cavalry skirmishes that made up the campaigns of the time, together with sieges of formidable fortresses. In the latter case, one of his opponents at Val-ès-Dunes, a rival for his title known as Guy of Burgundy, fled to his castle at Brionne. This was a stone hall (when most fortifications were still wooden constructions), on an island in the middle of the River Risle. Unable to attack it directly, William resorted to blockade and eventually, after three years, forced Guy to surrender and accept exile. In addition to internal threats, he was challenged on his southern border by Geoffrey, count of Anjou, who had gained control of the castle-towns of Domfront and Alençon. In about 1051, William was besieging Domfront, again by blockade, but was frustrated at the slowness

of the method. Seeking to break the deadlock, he secretly left the siege-lines with his mounted troops and force-marched across difficult terrain, at night, some 30 miles (50km) to arrive at Alençon at dawn. Its inhabitants were surprised, as were the defenders of the small fort across the river from the town. William called on them to surrender. This they refused, apparently offering insults instead. The duke ordered an assault and the fort was carried. He had the defenders mutilated, cutting off hands and feet. Although this seems harsh, according to the rules of war at the time their lives were at his mercy for refusing an offer of surrender. This exemplary punishment soon persuaded the citizens of Alençon that they had best surrender, too. Apparently the news ran swiftly back to Domfront, which also

The illustration of Duke William's Breton campaign (1064) epitomises French chivalric warfare. The Norman cavalry scoured the countryside to harry their enemy and force him into defensive positions. This is what is being depicted and not an apparent headlong charge at fortifications. Castles were reduced by more measured assault, fire – as shown here – or longer blockade. Conan, the Breton leader, symbolises his surrender by proffering the keys to Dinan to Duke William at lance-point. (Bayeux Tapestry. With special permission of the town of Bayeux)

surrendered. The story, which is told with approval by the duke's biographers, is the mark of the man. He knew when to be ruthless, as he was to show in his conquest of England, but he was not needlessly cruel. The end justified the means.

In 1053, William had to deal with the rebellion of his uncle, William of Arques, in his castle on the north-eastern borders of the duchy. This time the king of France was supporting the rebel against William, whose growing authority he had come to fear. As a French relief force with supplies approached the castle, the Normans sprang an ambush. The uncle surrendered and King Henry lost face. In the following year the king invaded the duchy in conjunction with Geoffrey of Anjou, anxious to bring his vassal to heel. While William adopted *Fabian tactics* against the king's army (avoiding a confrontation with forces which he knew were stronger than his own), his trusted barons attacked a French force at Mortmer, in the east of the duchy. They attacked the enemy camp at dawn, burnt it and captured many *knights*, whom they held to ransom. Henry retired hurt. In 1056, he tried again, leading his troops straight into the heart of the duchy. Travelling via Evreux, he marched to the coast to demonstrate his power. Turning to cross the River Dives near its mouth, his army discovered a causeway through the tidal waters. Half of the force passed over to the other side, then, suddenly, William launched his ambush to attack the baggage train and the rearguard. Impotent on the other side of the flood, King Henry watched his men, massacred, drowning, captured, while his supplies and treasure fell into Norman hands. It was said that he died of rage and disappointment soon afterwards (but since this happened in 1060, it must have taken some time to sink in). So, by the late 1050s, William was proving himself the pre-eminent warrior in northern France. In 1053, he had made an opportune match with Mathilda, daughter of Baldwin, count of Flanders. This both helped to protect his north-eastern flank and gave him a link to one of the richest counties, whose wealth

came from trade and the sea. This would prove helpful should he ever need a fleet. Baldwin later became the guardian of Philip, king of France, who succeeded his father as a minor. How convenient. There was now little chance of a threat from Paris.

During his years of fighting William had formed a body of loyal and dependable companions around him, men who liked his style and appreciated the rewards of his success. His closest friend was William fitzOsbern (the son of his murdered steward), but the years of the Conquest forged many more ties. Also, he had the support of his two half-brothers: Odo, made bishop of Bayeux while still a teenager, more warrior than prelate, and Robert, elevated to count of Mortain in 1058. Both were invaluable assistants in his military ambitions.

In the early 1060s, William took the initiative on the southern borders of the duchy. The death of Geoffrey of Anjou in 1060 allowed him to penetrate into the former Angevin protectorate of Maine, taking Le Mans in 1063. Another county that he sought to dominate was Brittany, a semi-wild region regarded by the Normans rather as the English regarded Wales. William planned a campaign in 1064, but he had an unexpected visitor that year: Harold, earl of Wessex. The scene was set for a conflict that would begin two years later.

William and Harold in Normandy

Sometime in spring 1064, Harold, earl of Wessex, made a trip to France. No one is entirely sure why. It may be that, as twelfth-century historian William of Malmesbury wrote, it was just a fishing trip that was blown off-course. Certainly he ended up in the clutches of Guy, count of Ponthieu, who promptly sold him on to Duke William. It may be that Harold was on an embassy to Normandy, as the Bayeux Tapestry suggests, at the direction of King Edward. That is certainly what the Norman sources (all written post-Conquest, of course) want us to believe.

Crossing the River Coisnon near Mont-St-Michel (an abbey fortress in the sea near the Breton frontier) some Normans became caught in the quicksands. Earl Harold, fighting as a hostage for Duke William, displayed his great strength and courage by rescuing them. The Norman sources give Harold full credit for his warrior virtues, and only criticise his faithlessness. (Bayeux Tapestry. With special permission of the town of Bayeux.)

Whatever the reason, Harold joined William on campaign, as was common for noble hostages at the time, and he served him well. The Bayeux Tapestry depicts how William defeated Conan, count of Brittany, his only reverse being before the fortress abbey of Mont-St-Michel. This lay just off the western coast of Normandy, at the base of the Côtentin peninsula. The Normans got into trouble amidst the tidal waters and sinking sands, and the Tapestry shows Harold's superhuman strength as he rescued men from drowning. In response, William

honoured the Englishman by knighting him – but there was a catch. In so doing the duke was asserting his superiority over the earl, making him his vassal. The Tapestry and other Norman sources portray Harold's oath, probably taken at several places in the duchy in front of a large audience.

Harold's oath

The most detailed description of what he promised comes from the account of William of Poitiers, Duke William's chaplain and devoted biographer. He states that Harold swore an oath of *fealty* (personal loyalty) to William and agreed to act as the duke's agent in England at King Edward's court, seeking to bring about William's succession; he would fortify Dover at his own expense and hand it over to a Norman garrison, as well as

ANSIERVNT :FLVMEN: COSNONI
hIC: hAROLD :DVX: TRAhEBA
DEARENA

entrusting other castles into the hands of the duke's *castellans*, wherever the duke should require. This represented the destruction of all that Harold and his father had striven for over three decades since the death of Cnut. However, there was a problem with the oath: an oath taken under duress was condemned by the Church and recognised by no one. Once Harold was released he was under no real obligation to uphold his vows.

There is also the question of how William justified his claim to the English throne. This could scarcely be by blood since he was illegitimate, and his closest connection was

The Latin rubric reads: 'Here William has given Harold arms'. This scene has been described as the knighting of Harold, but the ceremony had greater implications. The banner in Harold's left hand represents his lands, which he receives back from the duke having become his vassal. (Bayeux Tapestry. With special permission of the town of Bayeux)

through his great-aunt, Emma. One version of the Anglo-Saxon Chronicle ('D') does claim that he had visited England in 1051, to be offered the throne by Edward, but this is unlikely in the light of his commitments in the war with Anjou, and probably reflects a post-Conquest interpretation of events. William was a supreme opportunist, though, and did know that Edward retained much affection for the land of his exile.

Another card that William played stemmed from Edward's interest in Church reform. This was one reason why he had brought in Robert, a former monk of the principal ducal

abbey of Jumièges, not far from Rouen. Robert had been forced to flee when Godwine and his family revenged themselves for their exile in the previous year. He was replaced by Stigand, bishop of Winchester, an old ally of the Godwine clan and closely linked to the dowager queen Emma. Unfortunately for Stigand, he was initially unable to receive his *pallium* (a stole worn over his clerical vestments which symbolised his legitimacy in office) from the Pope. When he did eventually get to Rome, he was consecrated by a pope whose own election was denounced by his successors. As a result, and for holding the sees of Winchester and Canterbury 'in plurality', Stigand was 'excommunicated and declared deposed by no less than five successive popes' (D.C. Douglas). In 1066, William was able to claim that his mission to invade England was to restore the proper running of its Church and bring it back into communion with Rome. Norman sources state that through the auspices of Lanfranc, abbot of Bec, Pope Alexander II awarded Duke

Harold swears an oath to Duke William on holy relics, including, under his left hand, a reliquary from Bayeux Cathedral. The duke's biographer, his chaplain, William of Poitiers, claims that this involved helping William to become king of England, and fortifying castles for him, including the key site of Dover, to be held by Norman garrisons. The English sources are silent on the matter, however, and Harold could justifiably object that an oath made under duress was invalid. (Bayeux Tapestry. With special permission of the town of Bayeux.)

King Edward's death scene. In the upper part of the picture he is shown supported by his steward, Robert fitzWymarc, while the tonsured Stigand provides the final unction. The dying king's right hand touches Earl Harold's, symbolising the transfer of authority to the kneeling earl, while weeping Queen Edith crouches at Edward's feet. The Tapestry illustrates exactly the description provided by the 'Life of King Edward' written by a St. Omer monk at the queen's command. (Bayeux Tapestry. With special permission of the town of Bayeux)

William a banner to symbolise the justice of his cause, fighting in papal service. On the Bayeux Tapestry, Eustace of Boulogne is shown carrying a standard and pointing at William, who is removing his helmet. The three-tailed pennant does show a cross and four blobs, one in each quarter. This may indeed be meant to represent the papal arms of a cross and four small crosses, although the same design is found on the coins of the counts of Boulogne in the period. This may mean that they are merely Eustace's arms, or that he chose to put the symbol on his coins to record the honour he once had of bearing the papal banner.

Whatever the case, another Norman adventurer, Robert Guiscard, had received a banner from Pope Nicholas II in 1059, as symbol of being made duke of Apulia as a papal vassal. King William was to hotly deny this last point when it was raised by the *papal curia*. While the evidence for the awarding of a papal banner is cloudy, Norman sources certainly made of the invasion in 1066 what was to be known to later generations as a crusade. This could only help to undermine King Harold's position, as some in his kingdom would have said that to oppose William would be to oppose the will of the Vicar of Christ.

Preparations and motivations

Harold seeks the throne

Once back in England, Harold set about strengthening his own claim to the throne. His greatest potential rival was his brother Tostig, earl of Northumbria, but in the autumn of 1065 a rebellion broke out against this southerner in a fiercely independent northern shire. The likely causes included over-heavy taxation and the abuse of the legal system, as a result of which several Northumbrian notables died. Some of these may have been enjoying the earl's hospitality at the time, although other sources blame Queen Edith, his sister. Whatever the reason, Tostig found his hearth-troops murdered, his treasure plundered and himself expelled, while the natives chose Morkere as their earl. The revolt threatened to become a political revolution as the northerners marched south, gathering support as they went and undermining the stability of Edward's throne. The king was too ill to confront the rebels himself, and despatched Harold instead. The earl negotiated a peace which sent the northerners home satisfied but resulted in the exile of his own brother. Tostig was mortified, and took himself off to Flanders, to the court of his father-in-law, count Baldwin. Once there he plotted to return and claim the throne for himself. The whole affair was very shady and Harold came out of it with little credit. Even the *Vita Edwardi Regis* (Life of King Edward), a source favourable to the Godwinesons, since it was written for Queen Edith, suggests that stories abounded that Harold had himself fomented the rebellion against his brother. When charged with this he swore that this was not so, but the *Vita* comments that he had always been too free with his oaths.

As Edward lay dying at Christmas 1065, the *Vita* describes who was gathered around his bed: Queen Edith, warming his feet like a dutiful wife; Stigand, archbishop of Canterbury; Robert fitzWymarc, Edward's Anglo-Norman steward, and Harold. It was customary for a king to designate an heir on his deathbed, and Edward effectively had no choice. He died on 5 January 1066 and the next day Harold was crowned king in Westminster Abbey. He had thrown down the gauntlet and, in so doing, plunged England into over half a decade of warfare.

The contestants prepare

As the news spread that Harold had been crowned, his rivals began their preparations, and there were three of them. As well as the ambitious William of Normandy and the embittered Tostig in Flanders there was another adventurer who threw his hat into the ring. His name was Harald nicknamed 'Hard-ruler', a viking who had made himself king of Norway 20 years earlier after a career as a raider and mercenary that had taken him as far as Constantinople. His slender claim was apparently based on an agreement made by his predecessor, Magnus, with Harthacnut that whoever died first would inherit the other's territory. Of course, this did not happen, since Edward took the English throne in 1042. More to the point perhaps was Harald's ambition and the usual viking tendency to fish in troubled waters. After all, his son Olaf had taken part in the troubles of 1058, when Aelfgar fought for the second time to regain his earldom.

It is possible that Tostig sought Harald's help in the winter of 1065/66, but the sources for this are late and unreliable. Certainly, Tostig made the first move in 1066 when he sailed from Flanders just after Easter (late April) to the Isle of Wight. Presumably

King Harold's coronation with archbishop Stigand officiating. The scene further underlines Harold's unworthiness to rule, for Stigand was not recognised by Pope Alexander II. In his left hand the archbishop holds his *pallium* (a clerical stole that symbolised his ecclesiastical office). This is a visual reminder that he had been appointed by the 'anti-pope' Benedict VIII. By receiving the crown from an excommunicate cleric, Harold's status is shown to be invalid. (Bayeux Tapestry. With special permission of the town of Bayeux)

he was seeking to emulate his father's success in 1052. He then set out for Sandwich, but did not find the support he hoped for there and, on news of King Harold's approach, he sailed on up the coast to Lindsey (Lincolnshire). There the brothers Edwine of Mercia and Morkere of Northumbria drove him off, so that he was forced to take up refuge with Malcolm Canmore, King of Scots. Apparently Tostig had been deserted by most of his men and had only 12 ships with him, remaining in Scotland for the rest of the summer. It may have been at this time that he contacted Harald of Norway, for they arrived together at York in September.

Meanwhile, William of Normandy had also been making preparations. The Bayeux Tapestry is still the most informative depiction of how the duke gathered his forces, but it of necessity presents only snapshots of the events from January to October 1066. Nor should the viewer be misled into believing that William had all his ships built, as the Tapestry seems to suggest. It is difficult to know how large a fleet he assembled, but he would certainly have drawn upon the resources of his vassals, and the traditional obligations of the Norman seafaring towns. One contemporary source lists each lord's contribution, coming to a total of 776 ships, but this may be an exaggeration. In truth, we cannot know how many ships or men William gathered together. It is clear that, in addition to his own vassals, the duke raised troops with promises of wealth and lands in England. He also seems to have paid and fed his army over the long summer weeks when it was encamped near the mouth of the River Dives. Modern historians suggest that William's forces may have totalled 7,000–8,000 men, about 1,000–2,000 of them mounted, but these can be nothing more than guesstimates. Certainly, cavalry played an important part in his army, because the Tapestry shows many naval horse-transports carrying the knights' mounts as the fleet crossed to England.

The invasions of 1066 and King Harold's responses

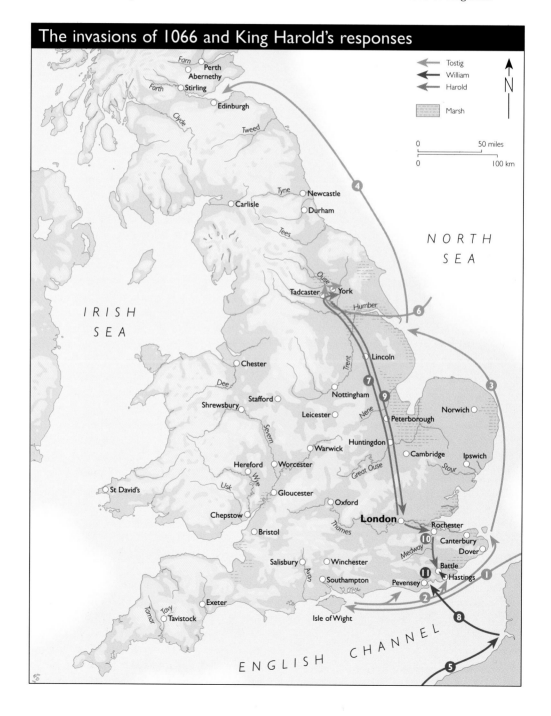

What is remarkable, though, is how long William waited before making the crossing. The traditional explanation for this, drawn from the Norman accounts, is that the winds were unfavourable. It is, however, extremely unlikely that the winds were contrary for almost three months. It is more probable that William waited deliberately – until Harold's land and sea forces' periods of service had expired. This is certainly what the Anglo-Saxon Chronicle (C) reports: 'When it was the Feast of the Nativity of St. Mary (8 September), the provisions of the people were gone, and nobody could keep them there any longer.' The fleet, returning

Horse transports crossing the Channel. Cavalry were such an important feature of French warfare that each knight had at least one, and often several mounts. There was nothing new about moving horses by sea, the Anglo-Saxon Chronicle describes vikings doing so in 892. There is also no evidence as to how the transports were constructed; most likely they were ordinary cargo vessels with improvised stalls. (Bayeux Tapestry. With special permission of the town of Bayeux)

to London, was dispersed and damaged by a storm. Just a few days after the English coast was denuded of defenders, William's fleet set out. It was then that the winds proved difficult (possibly as a result of the same storm which wrecked the English ships). The sailors had to make for a safe anchorage, and found it in a river estuary: the bay of the Somme. Whilst wind-bound at St-Valèry-sur-Somme, the Normans prayed to the town's patron saint for a fair wind. This took over a fortnight to arrive, but the Normans' despair was ill-placed because Harold Godwineson had to react to a northern invasion.

Harald of Norway's invasion

King Harald came with a fleet variously reported as being between 200 and 500 ships strong (modern historians suggest 300 as a likely figure). He met Tostig, who had only a few vessels, at Tynemouth on 8 September. They raided down the coast, sailed into the mouth of the Humber, then up the Ouse

OPPOSITE
1 April: Tostig attacks Isle of Wight.
2 Tostig raids along the south coast.
3 Tostig forced north and raids Lindsey.
4 Tostig sails on to Scotland.
5 September 11: William's fleet sails for England but is driven by storms into the Bay of the Somme.
6 Mid-September: Harald and Tostig's fleet arrives in the Humber. Their forces go on to defeat the English northern levies at Fulford Gate 22 September.
7 King Harold marches north and attacks the invaders at Stamford Bridge, 24 September. Harald and Tostig are killed.
8 Night of 28/29 September: William's fleet crosses the Channel to land his forces at Pevensey.
9 King Harold marches south and regroups his forces at London, early October.
10 Harold advances towards Hastings and takes up a position 7 miles (11km) north of the town.
11 William advances in the early morning of 14 October.

A carved antler horn from Sigtuna in Sweden, depicting a helmeted viking, is attributed to the eleventh century. The face, with its heavy moustache and beard, is topped with a conical *Spangenhelm* typical of the period. (Antivarisk-Topografiska Arkivet, Stockholm)

towards York, landing at Ricall, ten miles (16km) downstream of the city. It is difficult to estimate the numbers of the invading army. The viking longships of the era varied in size, but a common type of vessel would have 20 oars each side and two men to an oar, giving a crew of over 80 (allowing for the ship's master, steersman and other hands). Technically, at least, all these would be fighting men, although some would need to be detached to act as a ship-guard wherever the vikings decided to disembark. If their combined fleet really did contain 300 ships,

this suggests a fighting force of around 20,000 men, which seems too many for even the richest viking sea-king to support in this era, so it may be that the fleet was actually smaller.

There is even less evidence for the size of the army gathered by Edwine and Morkere to oppose the invaders. It would have been difficult to raise and sustain a force to equal that of King Harald, but clearly the earls thought they had a chance of winning, otherwise they would not have offered battle. There are no contemporary accounts of what took place during the battle, although Scandinavian *sagas* (long historical poems written down two centuries later) do provide some details. These details may be entirely spurious, of course. What we do know is that the best fighting men of both sides were probably equally well equipped, wearing knee-length mail coats, with helmets and shields to protect them. For offensive weapons, the vikings preferred long-handled axes, although these required the use of both hands, leaving the warriors unable to use their shields. It is likely that they were covered by other warriors using the spear and shield combination. The English front-line troops, after half a century of Danish influence in military affairs, were similarly armed. It may be that the back ranks were more lightly equipped, they being locally raised, part-time warriors who only served in times of national emergency. Such men may have had only spear and shield, lacking armour and possibly even a helmet (for which they would have substituted a leather cap).

The battle-formation adopted by men fighting in the Anglo-Scandinavian tradition was described by contemporaries as the *shield-wall*. Exactly what this meant has been a source of academic controversy for many years. Should we understand this as a tight-knit hedgehog of spears and other weapons? If so, how did it manoeuvre? (Presumably very slowly.) Also, the double-handed axes needed space to be swung for best effect, especially for the popular low-stroke, which came in under the shield and was designed to take off an opponents legs at, or below, the knee. Of course, it would have been perfectly possible to use the axe in a more restricted, hewing motion (such as is used in chopping wood), depending upon the strength of the shoulders and back alone, and without the additional momentum imparted by a wide swing. The well-armed warriors also carried swords, which again needed some space to be wielded to best effect. Even those of the highest quality steel, as many of the viking blades were, required impetus in order to cut through shield, armour, flesh and bone.

In addition to the close-quarter weapons, both sides used missile weapons: thrown javelins and clubs, but also bows. The vikings had a tradition of archery which valued the craft highly, and the bow was a useful weapon for naval combat, especially

before vessels could be brought together to allow boarding and subsequent hand-to-hand fighting. It is difficult to know whether archery was used only in the preliminaries to the battle, or throughout, to harry an opponent's lightly armoured back ranks. (These questions will be returned to in more detail in the description of the battle of Hastings.) This combination of factors suggests that the 'shield-wall' could not always have been a tight-knit formation, but may have opened up for movement and when the fighting developed into a series of individual or group duels.

The warrior ethos of the warring sides

In England, before the Conquest, it was generally agreed that in order to pay for the full military equipment of the era – horse and arms – for one man, an income equivalent to that derived from 5 *hides* of

A collection of eleventh-century axe- and spear-heads, found in the Thames near London Bridge, represent the type of weapons which the English and Scandinavians would have wielded in the battles of 1066. The heavy, asymmetrical axe-blade with the longer lower part, was known as 'bearded', for its fanciful similarity to a warrior's face. (Museum of London)

Two lively reconstructions of Norse warriors. The three figures (left) show a fully
equipped axeman and two unarmoured vikings. The baggy trousers are an
interpretation based upon Scandinavian stone carvings. (G.A. Embleton)
(Right) This 'Wolf-coat' wearer signals his adherence to a warrior cult by his fur cloak.
Mail armour was so expensive that many vikings could not afford it. At the Battle of
Stamford Bridge, the Anglo-Norwegians also lacked mail coats because they had left
them in camp following their victory over the northern English at Fulford Gate a few
days earlier. When King Harold appeared with his army, the unarmoured invaders
were at a severe disadvantage in the hand-to-hand fighting. (Paul Hitchen)

land was required (where a hide represented the income sufficient to support a peasant family). In the first half of the eleventh century this fighter – or potential fighter – was called a *thegn*. Even below this social rank men could find themselves required to perform military service. Under the old English state an obligation was placed upon every adult male to fight in defence of the kingdom. The force so raised was called the fyrd, and over the last generation historians have described it as the 'greater fyrd', with the term 'select fyrd' being reserved for the wealthier 'five-hide' warriors. In truth, it is difficult to find any references in contemporary sources to such a distinction. A more plausible explanation is that the warriors who went on campaign were those already used to service in the households of the great lords. There is the evidence of Berkshire Domesday, which presents the case that where five men possess land valued at one hide, four shall pay five shillings each (20s = one pound sterling) for the upkeep of the fifth one in war time. It is not impossible that this system was widespread throughout the old English shires of the kingdom, although the situation in the former Danelaw may have been different – but to claim the existence of a universal system in the light of this one example seems rash. In contrast with this apparently rational and national scheme of recruitment, there is an example from the customs of Chester, where one man was required to serve as long as his rations lasted. To the outrage of his lord, he turned up with a side of bacon, ate it, and went home!

It is very difficult (despite the last personalised example) to get an idea of the experience of the 'ordinary soldier' in war. There are references in Domesday Book to thegns (*tahinos* in Latin) killed at the battle of Hastings and their lands consequently being taken over by the victorious incomers. By reading the chronicle accounts, it is possible to gain some understanding of the hardship endured by the English defenders of the south coast in 1066, both the land army (*here*) and, especially, the naval forces (*scip here*) exposed

to the dangers of stormy seas. Yet we possess no personal memoirs such as are available for later periods of military history and which rise in volume from a trickle to a flood from the Napoleonic Wars of c.1800 to the massive conflicts of the twentieth century (really taking off in 1914–1918). To gain an understanding of what warriors were *supposed* to feel (which is an entirely different matter from what they actually felt) it is necessary to use a poetic source.

'The Battle of Maldon' is the title given to a poem about the English defeat of 991, in which their leader Byrthnoth was killed. Originally believed to be almost contemporary with the event, the poem is now attributed to the 1020s, after the Danish conquest, a time when patriotic Englishmen were mulling over how God had allowed them to be defeated. A key theme to the poem is treachery: the flight of some prominent noblemen leads many of the East Anglian force to believe that their commander has left the field. In fact, he has not, because Byrthnoth has been killed by a viking spear. The poem is then structured around the statements of warriors in his army as to why they should prefer death to flight. What is interesting about this structure is that it allows stereotypical representatives of all levels of society to stake their claim to their rank. Two of the individuals portrayed will serve to illustrate the point of how the warrior ethos was inculcated. The first is a noble youth from a prominent family, Aelfwine:

Remember the words that we uttered many a time over the mead [alcoholic drink], when on the benches, heroes in the hall, we made our boast about hard strife. Now may it be proved which of us is bold! I will make known my lineage to all, how I was born in Mercia of great race. Ealhhelm was my grandfather called, a wise ealdorman, happy in the world's goods. Thegns shall have no cause to reproach me among my people that I was ready to forsake this action, and seek my home, now that my lord lies, cut down in battle. This is no common grief to me, he was both my kinsman and my lord.

Swinging a double-handed axe left the warrior unable to use
his shield and so unprotected against a counter-thrust by spear
or sword. This scene has been interpreted to show axemen
working in pairs with a shield-bearer to cover them. They are
also using the weapon left-handed, which may be coincidental
or, possibly, an accurate depiction of a blow aimed so as to
attack an opponent on his left, unshielded side. (Bayeux
Tapestry. With special permission of the town of Bayeux.)

The second, Brihtwold, is an elderly
retainer who speaks feelingly of the attitudes
of a dependant:

*Minds must be harder, hearts bolder, courage
the greater as our strength grows less. Here lies
our commander all hacked down, the good man
in the dirt. Ever he must mourn who thinks to go
home from this battle-play. I am an old man. I
shall not leave, but I mean to die beside my lord,
by the man so dear to me.*

The vikings, too, had their heroic
literature, both short poems and the much
longer (and far later) sagas. King Harald was
both a poet and the hero of many sagas,
having an entire cycle dedicated to him and
his exploits. Recognition of the need for
bravery in battle could be a short epitaph,
such as that found on a Swedish rune-stone
for a certain Asbjorn: 'He did not flee at
Uppsala but fought as long as he had
weapons.' He had been killed in the battle
of Fyris, a great victory for the late tenth-
century Swedish king Erik over an invading
viking force. *Haraldssaga* records a battle
against Swein Estrithsson, king of Denmark:

*Eager-hearted Harald/ urged his men to
battle;/ no hope of peace he offered/ to Norway's
sturdy seamen./ Norway's famous war-king/
charged them to die nobly/ and not to think of
yielding; his men then seized their weapons ...
The two great war-leaders,/ shieldless, shunning
armour,/ called for thrust and parry; armies were
locked in battle./ Stones and arrows were flying,/
sword-blades were dyed crimson;/ all around,
doomed warriors,/ fell before the onslaught.*

There is a persistent myth, based upon the
writings of later medieval poets and chroniclers,
that there were amongst the vikings certain
warriors known as *berserkers*, who went into
battle in a drug- or religiously inspired rage. It
does not diminish the vikings' reputation for
ferocity in war one bit to abandon this fantasy,
for that is what it is. They went into the fight as
other men, steeling themselves for the fray. As
King Harald allegedly sang in his own death-
poem at Stamford Bridge, *We never kneel in
battle,/ before the storm of weapons/ and crouch
behind our shields;/ so the noble lady told me./ She
told me once to carry/ my head always high in
battle,/ where swords seek to shatter/ the skulls of
doomed warriors.*

Two invasions, one conquest

The battle of Fulford Gate

Harald's victory at Fulford seems to have been fairly swift. This is hardly surprising, since the vikings were much more used to fighting together than the majority of the English forces. The *Heimskringla* saga purports to describe the deployments. The fighting took place on the left (east) bank of the Ouse, with armies confined between the river and the dyke. Edwine led the English right, opposite Harald, who raised his 'Land-Waster' raven banner. On the left, Morkere's Northumbrians opposed their hated former earl, Tostig, and seem to have begun the fighting with a violent attack upon his flank. After an initial success, a

An eleventh-century English manuscript shows mounted warriors on the march. Although it does not prove either way whether the pre-Conquest English used cavalry in battle, it is a reminder that they were just as 'horsy' a society as that of northern France. According to the 'Laws of Cnut', an earl's *heriot* (royal death duty) included eight horses, and that of a thegn, one. The decision to fight on foot probably owed much to the tactical requirements of an encounter; although it is true that we do not possess any accounts of insular cavalry warfare to match those of Duke William's career. (By permission of The British Library, MS Cotton Claudius Biv f25)

viking counter-attack broke the English line with heavy loss, many of the defeated drowning in the river as they tried to flee. Both earls escaped but their force was scattered, leaving York open to the invaders. The battle took place on 20 September; four days later the city submitted to King Harald.

King Harold Godwineson's march

The victors were totally unaware that the English king was only half a day's march away. How had he managed this dramatic achievement? As has been explained, he had stood-down his forces along the south coast on 8 September, possibly the very day that Harald's fleet arrived off Northumbria. It seems to have taken him a week, upon hearing this news, to muster around him more than just his bodyguard of *huscarls*, whereupon he set off for York, marching distances of up to 25 miles (40km) a day. The distance from London is over 200 miles (320km), but by the evening of Sunday 24 September he had reached Tadcaster, only 15 miles (24km) from York.

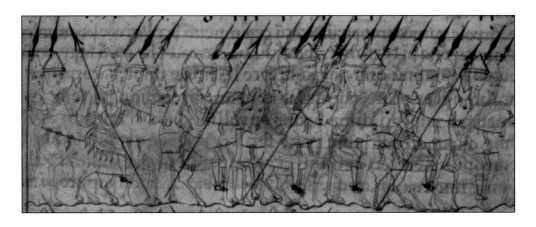

Harald and Tóstig felt so secure, they had set up camp just to the east of York, at Stamford Bridge, waiting for the exchange of hostages which was to confirm their arrangements with the citizens. They were completely taken by surprise when Harold's English army marched straight through the city and fell upon them. Although it is almost impossible to discover the exact site of the battle, it is believed to have taken place in the meadows to the east of the River Derwent, a tributary of the Ouse. Certainly, accounts of the fighting describe the English having to cross a small bridge, which was held by only one man. They were held up for a while by this brave individual, until a cunning Englishman found a small boat, in which he floated underneath the bridge and then stuck his spear upwards through its planks, so killing the defender.

This allowed the English to cross over and attack the Anglo-Norwegian forces. Once again, saga accounts provide all kinds of details of what took place, including King Harold riding up to the enemy line and engaging in a verbal exchange with Harald. The battle is then described as close-fought until the king of Norway took an arrow in his throat. Several historians have commented that this story, compiled much later, sounds more like a garbled version of Hastings. Also, there is the question, how did an experienced viking force, flushed with victory over the English only a few days earlier, allow itself to be overcome? One reason may be that the warriors had not sobered up after the victory celebrations. More significant, though, was the fact that most of the invaders had put aside their mail coats (the defender of the bridge being distinguished as still wearing his). This made them extremely vulnerable in the fighting. In addition, despite the saga descriptions, it is quite likely that they did not have time to form up properly before the English were among them.

One historical debate has revolved around whether the English fought mounted at

Stamford Bridge, as the sagas maintain. This has often been seen as an anachronistic interpretation based upon their authors' understanding of thirteenth-century warfare. If the English did fight mounted, though, it may be that some of them had simply not dismounted from the horses they had ridden on the march and simply charged straight into a mob of unarmoured and disordered men. Both Harald and Tostig were killed in the ensuing rout. The Anglo-Saxon Chronicle claims that there were only enough survivors left to fill two dozen ships from the huge fleet, who were allowed to sail home under the command of Harald's son, Olaf.

As a landing-place Pevensey provided both a large, shallow bay and an old Roman fort to act as a defended base. (English Heritage)

Harold Godwineson's victory was total. Displaying energy, initiative and determination, he had killed both his northern rivals and dispersed their forces. He had further enhanced his military reputation and provided a justification for his claim to the throne. Yet another threat remained, for even as his men celebrated the deaths of their old viking enemies outside York, a new untried invasion force was arriving 250 miles (402km) away on the south coast, and had to be confronted in its turn.

William's fleet crosses the Channel

When the wind turned favourable on 28 September, William's fleet set out after his flagship, which had a lantern at its mast. This was because the crossing was going to be by night and the duke was anxious to try to keep his ships together. In this, he was only partially successful, but the bulk of the fleet seems to have arrived at its intended destination. This was Pevensey, the site of a Roman fort which overlooked a large bay. The area is all reclaimed land now, but in the eleventh century there was a great expanse of water, spreading out into shallows and

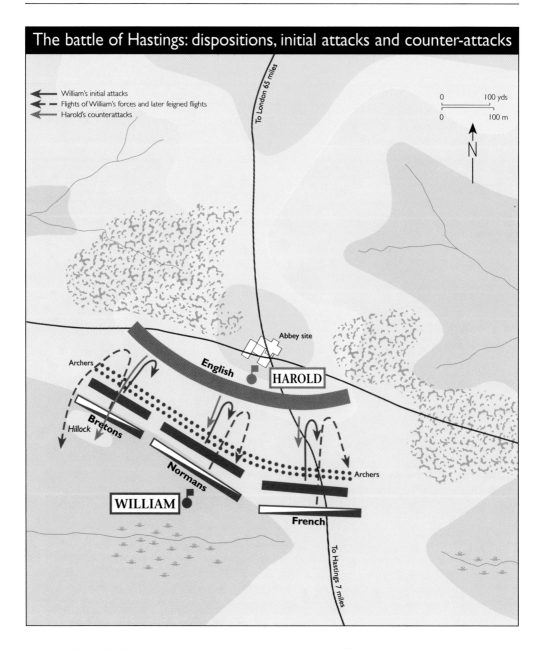

The battle of Hastings: dispositions, initial attacks and counter-attacks

marshland which formed a perfect harbour for shipping without deep keels. There was no resistance as the ships sailed in and disembarked men and horses, allowing William's troops to spread out, scouting and foraging. Pevensey's Roman walls were fortified, and a few days later, advancing to Hastings, William had a castle constructed there on a cliff. He now had a secure bridgehead on a hostile shore, although William of Poitiers alleges that an English

fleet of '700' ships was sent to cut him off. For the news of the Norman invasion had reached King Harold at York on about 1 October, and he responded as swiftly as he had previously. Once again he marched his forces rapidly against the enemy, spending several days in London before he set out for the south coast. Harold has been criticised for being too impetuous at this point of the campaign. In part this may have been because it was his lands that were being ravaged by the Norman troops, and his tenants whose homes were being burned and who were left destitute. We can assume that William well understood this and may have encouraged a harshness over and above the requirements of foraging. The king may also have sought to repeat the surprise attack that had worked so well in the north. He was facing a different opponent, though, one who was 'dug-in' and prepared for the English attack.

Marching south from London, Harold ordered that his troops muster at the 'old apple tree' on the heights now known as Caldebec Hill, about 8 miles (13 km) north of Hastings. This involved about half a day of normal marching, and the king's intention presumably was to gather the men

Two types of English warriors at Hastings. The well-equipped *huscarl* is swinging his axe below shield level to take advantage of an opponent at or below the knee. He has shouldered his kite-shaped shield to free his arms for best use of the two-handled axe. The Bayeux Tapestry shows many more lightly equipped Englishmen, who it has been suggested were members of the general levy, or *fyrd*. The charging spearman also carries a *seax*-knife at his belt. The crude stone axe is a throwing weapon. William of Poitiers describes a hail of these missiles in the initial assaults at Hastings. (Paul Hitchen)

of the south-east in addition to those he had with him. He would then have had a comfortable numerical superiority over William. But the duke, hearing of Harold's approach, set out early enough on the morning of Saturday 14 October to arrive by about 9.00 am that day. Harold's troops had advanced onto 'hammer-head' ridge, well protected on the flanks by woods and in front by a stream and marshy ground. He may have had only one-third to a half of his intended force available, so he took up a strictly defensive position, his shield-wall tightly packed into the confined position. All he needed to do was hold ground; it was up to William to achieve a victory.

Duke William's soldiers

The invaders of 1066 also possessed a warrior ideology. The hero of the *Song of Roland* also prefers death before disgrace, although, like Byrthnoth, he is criticised for the overbearing pride that led him to offer battle. The French epic poems of which the Song of Roland is the best known actually stress that a great warrior should be both '*sage et preux*' (wise and brave) and emphasise that knowledge

and prudence are also key qualities in a knight. Several authors assert that the Song of Roland was actually chanted by a minstrel who rode between the battle lines at Hastings, and one source gives his name as Taillefer. Whether such an event took place must be doubtful, but there can be no doubt that the knights in William's forces were imbued with the ethos of the poem.

Of course, not all the men who fought in the wars of the Conquest were part of the military elite. Their experience of warfare was inevitably different from their social superiors'. A poem written a century after Hastings, in the French of the period, does show an interest in such troops. The *Roman de Rou* is a celebration of Norman history, named after the first viking ruler of what became the eleventh-century duchy of Normandy. Its author, Wace, shows a great involvement with the ordinary soldiers, as two examples can show. In the first case, he is very interested in the role of the archers in

Disembarking the horses at Pevensey. There is no sign of the ramps or cranes used in later periods. The shallow draught of the transport vessels allowed them to be tipped onto their gunwales by pulling on the halyards supporting the mast. This enabled the horses to jump out, a risky, but apparently successful method. (Bayeux Tapestry. With special permission of the town of Bayeux.)

William's cavalry advances to battle. Although fine-looking animals with strong, curved necks, the horses were probably only 14–15 hands high (4–5 feet / 1.22–1.52m) at the shoulder. The knights ride with a straight leg, giving them a secure seat in the box-like saddles, to help withstand the couched-lance attack. This did not enable them to ride down determined infantry, though, as the myth of knightly dominance (supposedly begun at Hastings) has suggested. The square of studded leather, apparently on the knights' chest, is in fact the unlaced mail ventail (lower face-guard). For reasons of ventilation and communication this was only tied across the mouth in battle. (Bayeux Tapestry. With special permission of the town of Bayeux)

the invading army. He describes them as landing first from the ships at Pevensey and fanning out as a screen to protect the knights as they disembarked their horses. Their equipment is described in some detail, which is rare for the period: unarmoured, with leather caps (as they are shown on the Tapestry), with a hatchet or bill-hook hanging from their belts. At a time when only the knights are usually portrayed as warriors, this sympathetic description is unusual. The archers' role in the battle was to prove crucial. Wace also exemplifies the ordinary soldier's role by telling the tale of a *soudadier* (literally a 'shilling man'), the word from which modern English derives 'soldier'. Faced with a fearsome opponent, an Englishman swinging an axe who has already killed several men and decapitated a horse, the paid man proves himself worth

his hire by killing him. Although imaginary interpretations, Wace's insights cannot have been far from the truth for the ordinary fighting men in William's army.

The battle of Hastings

The duke deployed his forces in the traditional three 'battles' (divisions) described by their regional affiliations. So, on his left flank were the Breton troops led by their count, Alan. In the centre were the Normans, and to the right his French allies. The front line was made up of bowmen, followed by footmen armed with spear and shield, then his cavalry were held in reserve. William needed to break up the shield-wall before sending in his knights. At first, this seemed an unlikely result. Shooting uphill, the archers, together with some crossbowmen, saw their missiles either hit the shields of their enemies or sail over their heads. They then retired and allowed the spearmen to conduct the assault. The defending English sent down a barrage of missiles against them, described not as arrows (archers seem to have been mysteriously absent in their army) but as 'spears and weapons of every kind, murderous axes and stones tied to sticks'. The foot soldiers fell back in disorder, requiring the knights to charge up the hill.

The battle of Hastings: final attack and English collapse

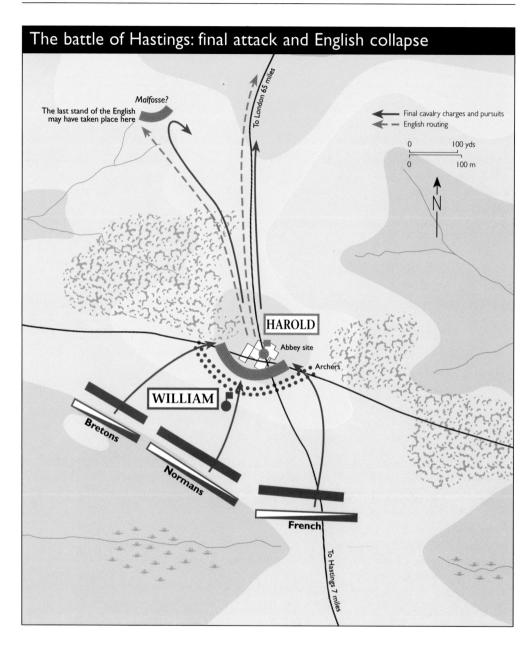

But William's cavalry were equally ineffective against the determined English. The huscarls, with their two-handed axes, were capable of cutting through any armour and even of decapitating the knights' horses. As a result, a general movement began to the rear, although the Bretons were blamed for starting the flight. As the left wing gave way the cry went up that William had been killed. Acting quickly to prevent a rout, the duke rode across the

front of his army, his helmet raised to show his face, shouting that he would not be beaten. On the English right, many men raced downhill in pursuit of the Bretons. Whether this was an intentional pursuit or not is uncertain, but once on the lower ground and in disorder, they found themselves counter-attacked and cut down by enemy cavalry. Some scrambled up to the top of a hillock (which can still be seen on the battlefield today) where they were surrounded and neutralised or killed.

This incident seems to have given William an idea as to how he could win the battle: by sending his cavalry against the hill and then withdrawing as if afraid. Norman sources describe two of these feigned flights which weakened the English line. As men left the shield-wall and rushed down the hill in pursuit, they were then counter-attacked on the level ground, surrounded and killed. The result of this tactic was that there were no longer enough defenders to cover the top of the ridge. As evening approached, Harold was struck in the eye by an arrow (although it was two generations later that a historian first attributed this to the duke's ordering the archers to shoot high into the air). The English faltered, and the mounted knights drove their tired horses into gaps in the shield-wall, cutting down the defenders, Harold amongst them. The king's death

precipitated a rout and, apart from a rearguard action at a still unidentified site ('The Malfosse'), the battle was over. A twelfth-century tradition has it that William vowed to build a monastery on the site, placing the high altar at the spot where Harold fell. This thank-offering to God became known as Battle Abbey, the ruins of which still stand on the hill.

The invading army seems to have had a large component of archers, if the Tapestry can be believed. Their tactical combination with the French cavalry won the battle in the end. Here, three figures are shown unarmoured, in leather caps, as the poet Wace describes them. The fourth figure has mystified historians, but he is probably a crossbowman. This is suggested by both his stance – he does not need to brace his feet apart like a bowman – and the much smaller 'arrows' (actually quarrels) which he holds in his left hand. Perhaps the Tapestry designer or creator was unsure of what a crossbow looked like, since they were a novelty in England at the time. (Bayeux Tapestry. With special permission of the town of Bayeux.)

ABOVE This reconstruction of a Norman knight, based on the Tapestry, gives a good impression of the relative size of man and horse, and how a skilled cavalryman managed his weapons, shield and excited mount at the same time. (Paul Hitchen)

RIGHT A crossbowman took much longer to reload his weapon than an archer, so this is why he needed some kind of protection against enemy missile-fire. His weapon is of simple construction, depending upon a horn or wooden 'nut' to hold the cord in place. A short wooden quarrel, with wooden or leather flights was then placed in the channel, allowing release when the serpentine trigger was pressed. (Paul Hitchen)

The march to London

ABOVE The English battle-line at Hastings, emphasising the close-order and weapons of the warriors. A hand-axe, club and many javelins are being thrown from the massed ranks. The sole archer may indicate a deficiency in this arm among Harold's troops. (Bayeux Tapestry. With special permission of the town of Bayeux.)

Harold's death and the dispersal of his army meant that William was the successful candidate for the English throne, but he had to make this good by getting himself crowned at Westminster Abbey. He did not advance on London immediately, however. He used an indirect approach, first marching east along the coast to Romney, where he routed the resistance, and then to Dover (21 October). This fortress, called the 'Key to the Kingdom' by a thirteenth-century historian, was a burh, but the example of Romney persuaded its defenders not to resist. William had it secured and ordered the construction of a castle within it (which was rebuilt in stone in the twelfth century and retained a royal garrison until 1967). After a week William left for Canterbury. The cathedral city was both the see of the archbishop and also a wealthy place. Stigand was not in residence. William soon pressed on to the Thames, but he could not or chose not to cross it with the city's fortified bridge held against him, and confined himself to

burning the suburb of Southwark. Within the city Edwine and Morkere were organising resistance around the only surviving English claimant, Edgar, a cousin of Edward, but only a teenager. William then marched upstream to Wallingford, some 30 miles to the west, where he took the submission of Stigand and ordered the construction of a castle within the impressive *burh*. He was also joined by reinforcements who had landed near Portsmouth and advanced via Winchester, the capital of Wessex and centre of English government at the time. Crossing the Thames at this point enabled the duke to swing around the Chiltern Hills and to approach London from the north, so cutting off any possible relief to the city. He ordered his troops to ravage the land at several strategic points during the campaign, and

TOP William rallies the troops at the crisis of the battle of Hastings, when it was believed that he had been killed. He has loosed his ventail and is raising his helmet to show his face. According to William of Poitiers he shouted: 'Look at me. I am alive, and by God's help, I shall win!' (Bayeux Tapestry. With special permission of the town of Bayeux.)

BOTTOM The death of King Harold. The full scene shows Harold twice, first wounded in the eye, and then, on the right, cut down by a horseman. The falling figure may once have had an arrow in his eye, but the stitching has been lost. A near-contemporary poem describes the actions of four men who killed the king, including one who slashed him on the thigh after he had fallen, incurring both dishonour and William's displeasure. This incident seems to be referred to in the picture. (Bayeux Tapestry. With special permission of the town of Bayeux.)

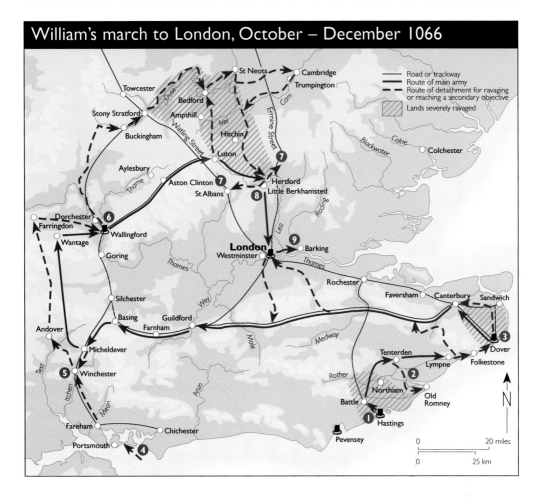

William's march to London, October – December 1066

this was one them. As the Norman army approached in early December, the English opposition in London could only perceive themselves as cut off from any support. There does not seem to have been any fighting (although one source claims that a siege took place), as the English establishment chose to make peace with the Conqueror (as it had done 50 years earlier). On Christmas Day 1066, William was crowned King of England. Norman sources claim that the coronation was performed by Ealdred, bishop of York, rather than the uncanonical Stigand, because the whole ceremony was about legitimising his rule. Even though he had been crowned and had accepted the submission of many great men – the northern earls amongst them – this did not mean that he really controlled his new kingdom. In essence, he only had mastery

1 15–20 October – William rests his army.
2 Reprisal raid against Romney.
3 Dover surrenders to avoid punishment; advance delayed by outbreak of dysentery 21–28 October, but castle constructed.
4 Reinforcements arrive from Normandy late October.
5 Winchester surrenders at end of October.
6 Mid-November, Thames crossing seized and castle constructed. Stigand submits.
7 Ermine and Watling Streets blocked to prevent relief reaching London.
8 Early December, remaining English leaders submit.
9 William crowned at Westminster on Christmas Day then retires to Barking.

over the south-east corner of the country, from Buckinghamshire to Kent. The battle of Hastings is often treated as if it *was* the Norman Conquest, but in fact there were many years of English resistance, Danish intervention and hard fighting before William could truly feel secure. The construction of three castles began in London, one in the north-west of the city, and two on the waterfront. One of these was Barnard's Castle (near the site of the present Blackfriars Bridge), which no longer survives. The other, built in the south-east corner of the Roman walls, grew to be one of the greatest fortresses in the kingdom, the Tower of London. In 1066, this was only a wooden fort behind a palisaded ditch and bank – the stone 'White Tower' was not begun until towards the end of William's reign, yet it marked the heart of Norman government from the very first.

The first year of William's rule

By January 1067, William's forces had been under arms for over six months and badly needed rest, so it is not surprising that he did not attempt any further campaigning. In fact, the first movement he made was back to Normandy as soon as the spring sailing season would allow, in March, taking his English prisoners on a triumphal tour of the duchy. He celebrated his victory at Easter, at the ancient abbey of Fécamp, being sure to invite French guests to marvel at the barbarous appearance and luxurious dress of his English captives. Behind him in England he left reliable lieutenants, such as William fitzOsbern, who began constructing a castle at Arundel (West Sussex), strategically sited to control the south coast routes, and Odo, bishop of Bayeux, whom he made earl of Kent. This county, crucially placed for connections to the Continent, had to be in competent and reliable hands: already, in 1067, there was an attack upon Dover. Somewhat surprisingly, perhaps, this attack came from Eustace of Boulogne, who had been William's ally in 1066 and his standard-bearer. There seems to have been a falling-out, and William of Poitiers does describe the supposed humiliation of Eustace in the 'Malfosse' reverse at the end of the Hastings battle. But there may be no more to it than that Eustace was keen to gain Dover (which he may have been attempting in 1051) in order to gain for

The coronation of King William. 900 years after the creation of the original embroidery, an English needlewoman set about reconstructing the lost end portion of the Bayeux Tapestry. William is shown with Ealdred, archbishop of York, who lacked Stigand's disqualification and proved a loyal supporter until his death in September, 1069. (Bayeux Tapestry finale, commissioned by Madeira Threads UK Ltd, Thirsk, North Yorkshire, embroidered by Jan Messent)

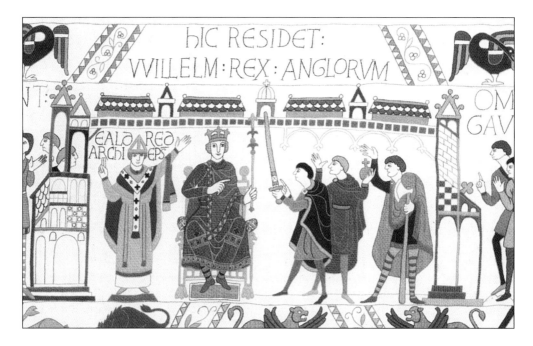

Eustace, count of Boulogne, has a prominent role on the Tapestry as William's standard-bearer, carrying the papal banner. He has only recently been identified as such. His nick-name: 'au grenons' meant to wear a moustache in the English manner (he was married to King Edward's sister), which was an unusual style in northern France at the time. Above his head is the remains of a name: E…TIUS (= Eustatius). The damage may be coincidental or related to his rebellion in 1067. (Bayeux Tapestry. With special permission of the town of Bayeux.)

himself a cross-Channel stranglehold of the Straits. Whatever the cause, the garrison remained loyal and drove off the attackers. William did not need Eustace's aid now, as he had in the previous year, and could draw upon naval resources and the wealth of a kingdom immeasurably more powerful than anything a mere northern French count could muster. (Eustace was later received back into favour, as his extensive landholdings in Domesday Book amply illustrate.)

Essentially, all was quiet in England during 1067 as William's new subjects struggled to come to terms with the incoming regime. The two incidents that did involve violence were both in the nature of local feuds. At Barking, in January, a northerner called Copsi persuaded William to make him earl of

Northumbria. Only a few weeks after reaching the Tyne he was attacked and killed by Osulf, whose family had previously held the title. Also, in the west, Eadric (later known as 'the Wild' for his outlaw activities) attacked Hereford castle in conjunction with the Welsh prince Bleddyn of Gwynedd, because he objected to the land-grabbing activity of its castellan, Richard fitzScrob. Neither of these incidents seem to have been directed against royal authority. Eadric was not punished, and when Osulf was killed by bandits, William allowed his family to retain the earldom in the person of Gospatric of Bamburgh.

Exeter rebels

Discontent did begin to rise, however, at the imposition of a heavy tax (the geld, which had been discontinued in 1051) to pay for the new king's military endeavours. Just as in the two cases already noted, it was in a region far from London that the first true rebellion began. The city of Exeter, in the south-west, was well fortified and its citizens independent in spirit. In addition, Harold's mother Gytha seems to have been sheltering there. William considered the revolt serious enough to warrant challenging immediately, and crossed the Channel at a dangerous time of year. He landed on 6 December 1067, the very day that Christ Church Canterbury burnt down. Although this was not ascribed to rebel activity, it was an ill omen. The king rapidly mustered forces, including the English levy, and marched into Devon in the depths of winter. Unsurprisingly, his forces suffered badly in the bitter weather, and Exeter's defenders were initially confident of withstanding a siege.

This lasted for 18 days, as William directed his men in a combination of assaults on the walls and attempts to undermine them. Although the royal army was unable to force its way in, the defenders obviously feared that this was inevitable and sued for terms. This enabled them to escape the consequences of a sack. William gave them generous terms, presumably because he needed freedom of action to operate elsewhere in the peninsula, subduing Devon and Cornwall before returning to keep Easter at Winchester. To ensure Exeter's continuing obedience he directed the construction of a castle inside its walls, under the command of Baldwin de Meules (the son of his murdered guardian, Gilbert of Brionne). William's concern was for loyalty, rewarded in the case of Baldwin, enforced in the case of the citizens.

William's strategy of constructing castles and providing them with a garrison was to prove crucial in finally quelling the English revolt. Yet, in the spring of 1068, the seriousness of opposition to his rule had not yet been borne in upon the king. On 11 May, Mathilda was crowned as his queen at Westminster, and the earls Edwine and Morkere were amongst the congregation; but their support was not to last. At some time over the summer, King Harold's son Godwine, who had taken refuge in Ireland with another brother or two, led a pirate fleet to attack the West Country. Landing at Avonmouth, they ravaged the countryside and attempted to storm Bristol. Repelled by its citizens, the raiders withdrew to Somerset, where the shire levy offered battle. Although its leader, Eadnoth the *Staller* (a companion of King Edward), was killed, the invaders were driven off and sailed away.

Soon afterwards William demanded the submission of the northern lords. When they tried to bargain instead, the king set out to establish his authority in the midland and northern shires. He did this, as at Exeter, by advancing into the regions and having castles constructed at important sites. At Warwick an enormous motte was raised, fortified and entrusted to Henry de Beaumont. This was intended to keep Earl Edwine quiet. William then advanced to Nottingham, appointing William Peverell as castellan there. Here he received the keys of York and a noble hostage as symbols of the citizens' loyalty. Clearly, the determination he had displayed at Exeter was bearing fruit. At York, the king ordered the construction of a castle (on the site of the present Clifford's

Tower), with Robert fitzRichard as its castellan and William's close companion William Malet as *sheriff* of Yorkshire. The royal army then turned south to Lincoln, where Turold was put in charge of the new castle. Returning to London, via Huntingdon and Cambridge, William had two more castles built there. He displayed confidence in the settlement so far by dismissing the stipendiary knights in his force and allowing some Normans to return home.

Clearly, William thought the north secure as well. Gospatric, earl of Northumbria, had fled to Scotland when the royal army was at York, so the king decided to replace him with a Norman, Robert de Commines. The new earl arrived at Durham with '500' knights in December 1068. A local chronicler asserts that his troops made themselves unwelcome because of their rapaciousness. Retribution was swift: only a month later Northumbrian rebels attacked the city, killing all the foreigners whom they could find (allegedly 900). Robert de Commines holed-up in the bishop's house, but he was burnt out and killed. The rebellion rapidly spread to York, where the castellan was killed while offering battle on 28 January, leaving William Malet to defend the castle. He managed to get a message out to William urging the king to bring a relief force. The severity of the threat was increased by the fact that the rebels had

OPPOSITE
1 Early 1067: William advances into East Anglia; a castle is begun at Norwich.
2 William returns to Normandy with hostages on a triumphal progress.
3 Autumn 1067: Eustace of Boulogne attempts to seize Dover, but is driven off.
4 Autumn 1067: Eadric the Wild raids Hereford with Welsh support.
5 January–February 1068: William marches to besiege rebellious Exeter, which is reduced after 18 days but only at great loss to royal forces.
6 Raids into Cornwall quell further opposition.
7 Summer 1068: Harold's sons launch raid from Ireland, but are driven off.
8 Summer 1068: York rebels.
9 William responds to northern rebellion, marches to York and quells revolt. Constructs castle en route and on the return to London.

chosen to be led by Edgar, supported by
Malcolm, King of Scots, and that they were
calling the young Englishman king.
William, who was in Normandy when the
news reached him, could scarcely have
faced greater danger to his position, and
acted swiftly.

The crisis year: 1069

Arriving in England, William mustered an
army and force-marched to York, catching the
rebels by surprise. He attacked and dispersed
them, killing hundreds of men, although
Edgar aetheling escaped to Scotland. To secure

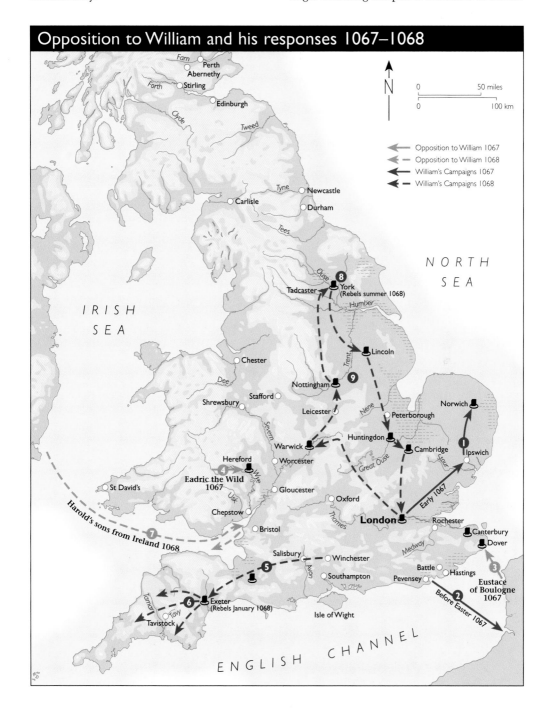

Opposition to William and his responses 1067–1068

the city, the king had its castle reconstructed and added another one. Gilbert de Ghent was made its castellan, but his contingent of Flemish troops proved unable to retake Durham unaided. William returned south to hold Easter at Winchester, and considered the situation still dangerous enough to require Queen Mathilda to retire to Normandy with their 17-year-old son Robert. In midsummer, Godwine Haroldsson returned 'with 64 ships' and landed in the mouth of the Tavy on the south Devon coast, probably seeking to seize the strategically important abbey of Tavistock. Count Brian of Brittany took them by surprise, killing many so that only a small force escaped to their ships. This is the last reference to the defiance of Harold's sons and their fate is unknown.

Meanwhile, in the north the rebellion had been resurrected by the arrival of a Danish fleet sometime in late August under King Swein's brother Asbjorn. This encouraged Earl Waltheof (the son of Earl Siward of Northumbria), Gospatric, Siward Barn and the leaders of York to call back Edgar to the city. On 19 September, the castle garrisons, in an attempt to clear the ground around their defences, accidentally set fire to the city. This resulted in the destruction of St Peter's Cathedral. The defenders could have done nothing worse to offend local sensibilities. When the Anglo-Danish force stormed the castles on 21 September, the garrisons were massacred without mercy, save for the castellans and their families, who were held to ransom.

Meanwhile, there had also been rebellions in the south and west. Montacute castle was besieged until relieved by Geoffrey de Coutances, who controlled Bristol. Exeter was also attacked, but was defended by its citizens, who this time remained loyal. The besiegers were caught between its walls and a relief force commanded by William fitzOsbern and scattered. On the Welsh border, Eadric the Wild, the men of Chester and Bleddyn of Gwynedd attacked Shrewsbury and burnt the town. The castle garrison defied them though, and when the attackers moved on to Stafford, the story was the same. King William, who

had been hunting in the Forest of Dean (near Chepstow), was well placed to deal with their revolt on his march north. He had instructed his half-brother Robert of Mortain to counter the Danish threat in the north. Their fleet was based on the south bank of the Humber at the Isle of Axholme but, because they seem to have destroyed the bases of the English fleet, the royalists were limited in their options. They did succeed in preventing the invaders from ravaging but could not deliver any retaliation. Autumn rains delayed William's arrival, apparently holding him up for three weeks until one of his knights discovered a ford across the River Aire. Despite a contested crossing, the royal army finally reached York to find it undefended. The English rebels had withdrawn and the Danish fleet was in the Humber and unreachable without a fleet, which William lacked. The king was forced to pursue the old policy of paying the Danes to go away, but he stayed in York. This was unprecedented, and a firm statement that the north was just as much part of his kingdom. To increase the symbolism, he had the ceremonial regalia brought to the city so that he could keep Christmas in state.

The harrying of the North

That there was more to ruling than display was made clear by his other actions. In a famous passage, the Anglo-Norman chronicler Orderic Vitalis describes his revenge against the rebellious region:

He himself continued to comb forests and remote mountain places, stopping at nothing to hunt out the enemy hidden there. His camps were spread out over an area of a 100 miles [160km]. He cut down many in his vengeance; destroyed the lairs of others; harried the land and burned homes to ashes. Nowhere else had William shown such cruelty. Shamefully he succumbed to this vice, for he made no effort to restrain his fury and punished the innocent along with the guilty. In his anger he commanded that all crops and herds, chattels and food of every kind should be brought together and burned to ashes with consuming fire, so that the whole region north of Humber might be stripped of all means of sustenance. In consequence so serious a scarcity was felt in England, and so terrible a famine fell upon the humble and defenceless populace, that more than 100,000 Christian folk of both sexes, young and old alike, perished of hunger.

This 'Harrying of the North', although feelingly condemned by the monastic chronicler for its brutality, was a standard procedure of warfare in the eleventh century and seems to have achieved its objective. William's operations after he had celebrated Christmas are unclear, but may have been conducted as far north as the Tees, and even to the Tweed. Certainly, he took the submission of Gospatric of Bamburgh (whose fortress lay just south of the Tweed), as well as Waltheof and other northern lords. Unfortunately for William, the aetheling Edgar escaped once again, and while he remained unreconciled the English rebels still possessed a standard-bearer for revolt.

Despite the winter weather, the king's enthusiasm for campaigning was undiminished. He was still concerned about his western frontier, which now lay on the other side of a mountain chain – the Pennines. It was at this point that there seems to have been a mutiny against William. The Norman chroniclers ascribe this to the weakness of 'the men of Anjou, Brittany and Maine' – everyone, in fact, except the Normans. Even if this represents an attempt to cover up the truth of more widespread discontent, the fears of the army were entirely justified. The passes of the Pennines regularly fill with snow in January and February, and it seemed to the soldiers that cavalry had never traversed these routes before. Many of the knights' horses sank into bogs, and only served to be eaten as other supplies vanished. The weather was foul – lashing rain and hail drove into the faces of the exhausted men. Only William seemed unaffected, leading with superhuman energy. He led his men on foot – a remarkable statement of solidarity with the foot soldiers in a society where riding conferred the status

of nobility. He promised that those who kept with him would be lavishly rewarded, while those who lagged behind would be ignored.

Eventually, he did reach Chester, and had a castle constructed within the south-western corner of its Roman walls. His presence made a powerful statement against the Welsh princes, who always sought to exploit weaknesses in English royal power. Roger de Montgomery had already raised a castle at Shrewsbury which, together with the older foundation at Hereford, helped to secure the *Marches*. William moved southwards and Stafford was also (re)fortified to provide a defence against the western rebels, as the king reasserted his authority over Mercia. After moving further south, the royal army was dismissed at Salisbury. Apparently, different treatment was meted out to its soldiers depending upon how loyally they had served in the winter campaign. According to Orderic Vitalis, those who had performed well were rewarded with money and lands, but the men who had been involved in the near-mutiny were retained for another 40 days. If this is true, then the significance of the length of time chosen was that it was the customary obligation of military tenants to their lord. In effect, by this punishment William was declaring that only after this period had expired was he satisfied that he had received his due service. This was a powerful message to any vassals – nobles and knights – who thought they could sell their ferocious monarch short in provision of the military duties that were essential to the confirmation of the Conquest.

A new administration

In hindsight, by crushing the northern revolt and neutralising the Danish threat William had secured his throne. His ruthlessness in the winter of 1069/1070 meant that never again would there be a general rebellion against his rule. At Easter, he was able to bolster his legitimacy by having himself crowned by a papal legate, Ermenfrid of Sitten. One of William's justifications for his

Opposition to William and his responses February–October 1069

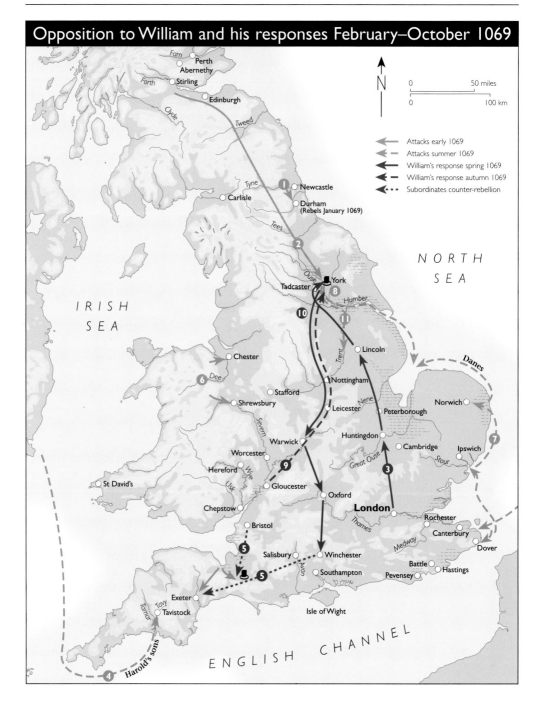

1 Durham rebels January 1069, Norman garrison slaughtered.
2 Rebellion spreads to York where the castle is besieged.
3 William marches north and disperses the rebels. He adds a second castle to its defences.
4 Midsummer 1069: Godwine Haroldson attacks Tavistock; his force is surprised and dispersed.
5 Summer 1069: Montacute Castle and Exeter attacked;

besiegers dispersed by relief forces from Bristol and Winchester.
6 Summer 1069: Eadric the Wild leads an attack on Shrewsbury, burning the town. Serious rebellion in the borders.
7 August 1069: Danish fleet appears off the east coast and works its way north.
8 September 1069: Danes storm York, which is badly damaged by fire; the cathedral is destroyed.

Opposition to William and his responses 1070

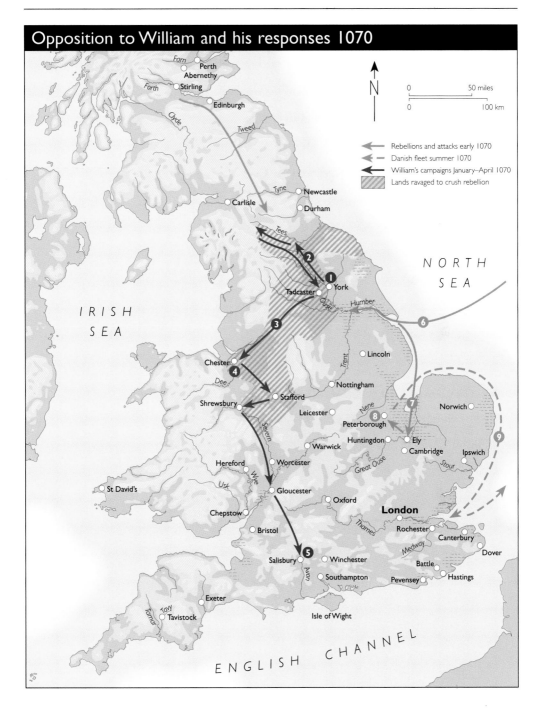

9 William marches north from Forest of Dean.
10 William delayed by river floods, but arrives at York and defeats rebels.
11 Danes retire to base in Isle of Axholme.

ABOVE
1 William spends Christmas 1069 at York.
2 January 1070: Norman forces advance into Northumbria, devastating the land.

3 February 1070: William crosses the Pennines to attack Chester.
4 Shrewsbury and Stafford relieved by royal forces.
5 Before Easter: Royal army dismissed at Salisbury.
6 Spring 1070: Swein of Denmark arrives to join his fleet.
7 May? 1070: Danes move to Ely; Hereward in revolt.
8 May 1070: Danes sack Peterborough; paid Danegeld to leave in June.
9 Route of Danish fleet home.

Harrying the land. Again a scene from before Hastings, but particularly applicable to the events of 1069–70 during William's 'Harrying of the North'. 'He cut down many in his vengeance; destroyed the lairs of others; harried the land and burned homes to ashes' (Orderic Vitalis). These harsh measures were taken to root out the last vestiges of resistance to the new regime. (Bayeux Tapestry. With special permission of the town of Bayeux.)

invasion was that the English Church needed reforming (although it is uncertain whether this was actually his policy in 1066 or a product of the historical writing of the 1070s). Certainly, he took measures against the English abbeys over the Lent of 1070, depriving them of their wealth. This may have been because the English nobility used the monastic houses as refuges for their riches – effectively using them as banks – and the king was determined to prevent the financing of further opposition. In addition, the presence of a papal representative enabled him to make changes to Church personnel – replacing politically unreliable clerics with his own men. Archbishop Stigand, an old ally of the Godwine dynasty, was deposed and replaced with William's choice: Lanfranc, a former Italian lawyer who

had become the abbot of the Conqueror's personal foundation of Caen and who had a reputation for administrative efficiency. The arch-see of York had become vacant the previous autumn, when Archbishop Ealdred had died just a few days before the city was stormed in September. The post went to Thomas, one of William's chaplains and so a close confidant. There were many other changes in ecclesiastical and monastic posts across the country. For society at the time, these were not just spiritual matters, but had serious political and financial implications, because senior clerics were effectively the civil servants of the royal government.

Contemporary sources recall the impact that the Conquest had upon the religious houses. William's requirement that they provide military service from their estates was regarded by many clerics, and especially monks, as a novel and unwelcome imposition. Yet how else was the king to deploy the resources of his realm against potential threats? Generally, those institutions that were compliant with the new regime were less heavily burdened than those in regions which displayed resistance. Yet even the important see of Worcester, which was retained in the hands of a highly regarded English bishop, Wulfstan (whose reported miracles led to his *canonisation* in the next century), had to fulfil its military quota. In the early years, just after the battle of Hastings, knights were quartered directly upon the monastic church of Worcester. This led to the almost comic sight of the saintly bishop sitting at table amongst his guests and vassals, as was his duty as a secular lord, abstemiously partaking of the monastic diet while around him the military men were gorging themselves and swigging back drink in the accustomed manner. At Abingdon, the abbot found himself responsible for garrisoning the new royal castle at nearby Windsor, strategically placed at a crossing of the Thames. Initially, he too had to retain knights in his household, but once peace settled upon the kingdom he was able to support his military tenants by granting them lands from the monastery's estates. Technically, this was in breach of Church law, yet in the changed times following 1066 the old English institutions had to grin and bear it.

Worse still was the situation of those abbeys that found themselves on the 'front line' of continuing English resistance. In 1070–71, this was to be found in East Anglia, where the Wash – essentially a great inlet of the North Sea – and extensive marshes made it possible for resistance to thrive even in the face of increasingly overwhelming royal power. A string of abbeys from north to south – Peterborough, Ramsey and Ely – became the fortresses over which the royalists and rebels fought. Peterborough's abbot, Aelfric, had already been removed in 1069, not least because he was the brother of Bishop Aethelwine of Durham (who had been implicated in the northern revolts of 1068 and 1069). His successor, Brand, sought confirmation from Edgar and, when he died in November 1069, William made sure that he had a loyal man in place. His choice was Turold, a pugnacious character from Malmesbury, the Conqueror allegedly quipping, on his selection, that since he behaved like a knight he might as well go

where the fighting was. Apparently he turned up to his new appointment accompanied by 160 knights (a veritable army by eleventh-century standards) – much to the disgust of the local inhabitants.

Hereward and the last English resistance

East Anglia became the last bastion of English – and Danish – resistance, based around the abbey of Ely. This was not entirely due to the feelings of the monks, but because a local nobleman – who was to pass into legend as Hereward the Wake – seized it in the summer of 1070. By that time he and his men had already sacked Peterborough (2 June) in anticipation of Turold's arrival. This was also in expectation of the appearance of the Danish fleet. The vikings had lain in the Humber all winter, but in the spring of 1070 they had been reinforced by ships under the personal command of the Danish king, Swein Ethrithson. In fact, it was his brother Asbjorn, who had not exactly distinguished himself in the previous year, who led his forces south into the Fens. This was classic viking terrain, where their shallow-draught ships could operate and raid at will. All they needed was a defended base, and this Hereward could provide for them. His seizure of Ely could have produced a serious threat to William, but once again the king chose to buy off the Danes, who returned to Scandinavia at the end of June.

This left Ely as the sole remaining centre for the English rebels, but it was not going to be an easy nut to crack. Although low-lying, the region today is dry land as a result of the extensive drainage programmes begun by Dutch engineers in the seventeenth century. Six hundred years earlier, the region of the Fens was more like a sea with scattered islands, although it was a shallow sea that in dry seasons was more accessible to land-movement. The name Ely is Old English for 'Eel Island', and a glance at the map shows clearly how defensible it was and how easily supplied by ships. It is also only 15 miles

(24km) from Cambridge (which was fortified with a castle by King William in 1068), not much further from Huntingdon (similarly provided), and strategically placed so as to allow a Danish force to move northwards to Lincolnshire and Yorkshire, east into the Midlands or south towards London. The abbey itself contained stone buildings, which were easily made defensible and could be relied upon to resist the siege weapons of the era.

This is why it was crucial to William to remove the Danes from the scene. Yet, even with them gone by midsummer 1070, he needed to muster extensive land and sea forces to deal with the English rebels. Although there are few details, it seems that attempts by subordinate commanders met with disaster. Several charters are dated with the ominous clause, 'when William Malet went into the marsh'. Since he was one of William's most reliable men (and the hero of the defence of York when cut off and surrounded in 1069), this loss must have represented a severe blow both to the king's strategic aims and his prestige. Ely seems to have become a beacon of resistance as much as a last refuge, for according to the Anglo-Saxon Chronicle, in 1071 'earl Edwin and earl Morkere fled away and travelled aimlessly in woods and moors until Edwine was killed by his own men and Morkere went to Ely by ship'. The phraseology may seem strange, but what the annalist is saying in his reference to woods is that the two last powerful earls of Edward's reign had become silvatici (literally 'woodsmen'), the term used for rebels like Eadric the Wild before them. What caused the Mercian earls to despair is nowhere stated by contemporary chroniclers, but it probably had to do with the seizure and reallocation of midland estates by the incoming Normans and their allies. Deprived of landed tenants from whom they drew their military and financial support, they may have considered that the game was up for them – although another habitual rebel, Earl Waltheof, was actually pardoned and seems to have made his peace with the new regime, also marrying Judith, a niece of the Conqueror.

Other notables named as congregating at Ely were Siward Barn and Bishop Aethelwine of Durham 'and many hundred men with them', according to the Anglo-Saxon Chronicle. Sources for what turned out to be the final flaring of English resistance are sparse, although materials compiled in a twelfth-century Latin romance of Hereward's life are believed by some historians to derive from evidence much closer to the events.

King William's approach to the problem was to launch a combined assault from land and water. He gathered a fleet which sailed down the river Ouse from the Wash and established a blockade of the island. This proved insufficient as a threat, so the royalists sat down to a prolonged siege. In order to assault the abbey it proved necessary to construct causeways through the marshes in order to allow access for the besiegers and, later, siege equipment to be brought against the abbey's walls. The *Gesta Herewardi* provides some details as to how this was achieved:

[William] moved his whole army to Aldreth where the surrounding water and swamp were narrower, the breadth there extending to four furlongs [880 yards/800 m]. Having brought there tools and fitments of timber and stone, and heaps of all kinds they built a causeway through the swamp, although it was narrow and quite useless to them. Moreover, close to the wide river near this place, that is to say Aldreth, they assembled in the water large tree-trunks joined together with beams, and underneath tied whole sheep-skins, flayed and reversed and fully inflated so that the weight of those going over might be better borne. When this was finished such a multitude rushed onto it all at once, greedy for the gold and silver and other things, not a little of which was thought to be hidden in the Isle, that those hurrying in front were drowned together with the road itself they had made. Those who were in the middle of the company were swallowed up in the watery and deep swamp as well. A few of those who were following at the rear got away with difficulty, flinging down their weapons, wallowing in the water and making their way through the mud. Thus in this way, with hardly anybody pursuing them, great

The Ely campaign 1070–1071

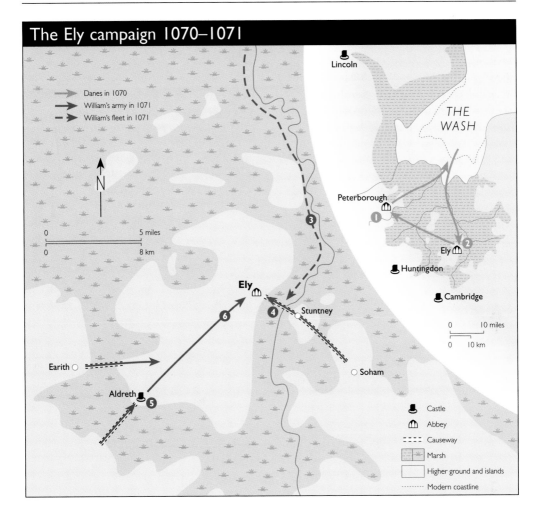

Legend:
→ Danes in 1070
→ William's army in 1071
--→ William's fleet in 1071

N

0 ——— 5 miles
0 ——— 8 km

0 ——— 10 miles
0 ——— 10 km

Lincoln

THE WASH

Peterborough 1

Ely 2

Huntingdon

Cambridge

Ely

6   4   ○ Stuntney

Earith ○

○ Soham

Aldreth 5

🛡 Castle
🏛 Abbey
- - - - Causeway
▨ Marsh
☐ Higher ground and islands
········· Modern coastline

numbers perished in the swamp and waters. And to this day many of them are dragged out of the depths of those waters in rotting armour. I have sometimes seen this myself.

Although this dramatic account is not contemporary, it is probably not an inaccurate description of William's first assault. The author is almost certainly mistaken in choosing Aldreth as the site from which it was launched, however. It is far more likely that it came from Stuntney, close to the abbey, and that the construction of the Aldreth causeway was the second option, for Aldreth lay at the other end of the island, half a dozen miles away from the defended enclave. Clearly the raft-cum-pontoon bridge was not going to work, so the king ordered a siege castle to be built at the end of each

1 May – June 1070: Danes sack Peterborough then leave.
2 Ely successfully defended against Norman forces..
3 Summer 1071: William's fleet cuts off relief from the sea.
4 Probable first attack on Ely; it fails.
5 Castle constructed to defend causeway.
6 Advance on abbey with combined assault from ships of the fleet and small boats leads to English surrender.

causeway. This enabled his men to defend the constructions. The romance continues:

Then when the war-engines were prepared as he had arranged ... the king began the attack, leading his entire army to Aldreth. He had also brought heaps of wood and stone and all materials for building ramparts there. And he ordered all the fishermen in the district to come with their boats to Cottenham so that they could ferry across what had been brought there and construct mounds and hillocks at Aldreth from the top of which they might fight.

Surrounded, and with no hope of victory, the defenders either slipped away by boat, as Hereward was reputed to have done, continuing his rebellion 'in the great forests of Northamptonshire', or surrendered to the royalists. William's ingenuity and determination had paid off. Those who could not stomach his rule fled abroad, like Siward Barn, who ended up in the eastern emperor's Varangian Guard in distant Constantinople; the rest submitted. William faced no more rebellions against his rule that were inspired by a sense of loyalty to the old English line, although troublesome barons were always capable of insurrection, as in any kingdom.

His last task was to bring in Edgar aetheling. This was part of the motivation for his final campaign of the Conquest, against Malcolm, King of Scots. His court had provided refuge for the young prince on several occasions since 1066, and the Scots continued their traditional policy of raiding the northern English shires, attacking in 1070. So, in a repetition of his 1071 campaign but on a much greater scale, William conducted a combined operation against Scotland. His army marched up the east coast, shadowed at first by the fleet, offshore. With his much smaller resources, Malcolm could not face veteran and confident troops in such force. The army had to march inland, and crossed the Firth of Forth at Stirling as the Scots retreated before them. William was reunited with his fleet at Abernethy, on the Tay, and here the King of Scots made his submission. Although this was not the end of Scottish raiding, the campaign assured William's status as the most powerful ruler in the British Isles. During the rest of his reign he had plenty to keep him busy, expanding and protecting his continental possessions. Apart from the crisis year of 1085–86, when a new Danish invasion threatened, he did not often feel the need to be present in his new kingdom and left it in the hands of his regents and deputies to rule over the last 15 years of his reign. Then, as he rode through the burning ruins of Mantes, in August 1087, his horse stumbled on the hot embers. By now extremely corpulent, William was thrown violently against the high pommel of his saddle. The blow caused an internal rupture, from which he died a few weeks later (9 September). However inglorious his death, his reputation as a great soldier was secure.

Viking legend, English 'patriot', and two Norman earls

Harald Hard-Ruler, King of Norway (1015?–1066)

Harald fought his first battle in 1030, aged about 15, at Stikelstad, near Trondheim, attempting to restore his uncle Olaf to the throne. Olaf (later St Olaf) was killed and Harald was wounded, fleeing eastward to Sweden and then to Russia. He was welcomed by Grand Prince Jaroslav of Kiev, whose wife was Swedish, and who valued Scandinavian links. Harald served a military apprenticeship, fighting in the Polish campaign of 1031, and then against other enemies of Kiev: the Byzantines, Estonians and *steppe nomads*. He also made an impact on Jaroslav's daughter, Elizaveta.

In about 1034, Harald moved on to Constantinople to serve in the Byzantine emperor's famous Varangian Guard, made up of Scandinavian and Rus 'axe-bearers'. He campaigned in Asia Minor, expelling the Arabs (by 1035) and even reaching the Euphrates. From 1038 to 1041, he served under George Maniakes in the reconquest of Sicily until the famous general was recalled and imprisoned by a jealous emperor. Coup and counter-coup saw Harald himself in jail for a while, on charges ranging from withholding booty to rape and murder. Released in mid-1042, he soon returned to Kiev and married Elizaveta.

In 1046, he sailed for home as a rich and renowned warrior. On the way he met up with Swein Estrithsson, who was trying to establish his claim to the throne of Denmark against Harald's nephew Magnus, now ruling in Norway. After initially fighting Magnus, Harald bought peace with his enormous fortune. When Magnus conveniently died in 1047, Harald was the natural successor, spending the next two decades consolidating his rule and engaging in a raiding war with

Denmark. Defeated in naval battle by Swein in 1049, Harald tried again in 1062. In another naval encounter at Nisa, the ships of both sides were roped together to form a fighting platform, although Harald kept a mobile reserve which sailed around the Danish fleet. Attacked from the rear, the Danes fled, losing many vessels but saving their men, among them the king. A peace treaty followed in 1064, for Harald now had his eyes on a greater prize: England. Harald's resources meant that a bid for the crown was well within his grasp. Fate decided otherwise and he died in battle, remembered for his bravery, ruthlessness, wealth and a talent for poetry, like the sagas which record his own deeds.

Hereward 'the last English rebel' (fl. 1060s–1070s)

Made famous by the great Victorian novelist Charles Kingsley (amongst others), as 'Hereward the Wake', legends grew early about this obscure thegn. The twelfth-century Latin text *Gesta Herewardi* describes his outlawry as a youth and adventures in Flanders (some of which may actually be true), Cornwall and Ireland (which are not) before returning home. There he discovers that his brother has been murdered in revenge for killing two Frenchmen, so he takes up arms against the invaders. After a series of incidents, including a rescue from prison by his men worthy of a Hollywood 'Robin Hood', King William is represented as being so impressed by the Englishman's chivalry that he pardons him at the end of the poem. This 'happy ending' conceals, though, the reality of the expulsion of the landed gentry of which Hereward was a part.

Hereward the Wake and his men attack the Normans. In later times perceived as an English hero, he was seen as a rebel and a bandit by the Norman regime and ended his days as an outlaw in the forest. (Ann Ronan Picture Library)

Domesday Book records that he held three manors in Lincolnshire worth 40 shillings (£2) each, yet on two occasions states that he did not possess some of his estates because of his 'flight' into outlawry. This may have reflected his involvement in the rebellion of 1069, perhaps prompted by an attempted takeover of his land by the invaders. Ogier, who appears in the *Gesta* as a main opponent, is probably Ogier the Breton, later possessor of two of the manors named. The third manor went to Frederick, who was killed by Hereward in 1070. This made him a powerful enemy, for Frederick's brother-in-law was the Norman noble William de Warenne, castellan of Lewes in Sussex and close to the king. Hereward held lands of Peterborough abbey, and was involved in the sacking of the house when the Danes came in the summer of 1070. Since he had such a dangerous reputation, only Ely could give him any refuge, and its

defenders did well to hold out against the royal forces for as long as they did. After the island fell in mid-1071, Hereward escaped to the forest of *Bruneswald*. This can be identified with Leighton Bromswold, the Northamptonshire estate of his companion-in-arms, Thorkell of Harringworth. His eventual fate is unknown.

Roger de Montgomery, earl of Shrewsbury and Arundel (?–c.1093)

Although his birth date is unknown, Roger was a close contemporary of Duke William, his cousin and companion in war since at least the siege of Domfront in c.1048. Marriage into the Bellême family made him one of the richest lords in Normandy, controlling castles and lands along the sensitive southern border, as well as his family estates in the heart of the duchy. As a most important vassal, Roger advised the duke on his invasion plans at Lillebonne, and is one of only a handful of men praised by William of Poitiers for his valour at Hastings.

The Conqueror displayed his trust in Roger by making him earl of Shrewsbury in about 1071, where his task was to contain and subjugate the Welsh. He was responsible for constructing the city's castle, along with many others, including one at Montgomery in southern Shropshire (although the present stone castle is from Henry III's reign). These fortifications both defended the frontier and provided bases for making inroads into Welsh territory, his son Hugh leading raids as far as Ceredigion and Dyfed. Such was the range of his responsibilities that he was twice an earl. He also constructed Arundel Castle in Sussex as part of the south-coast defences, based upon groups of estates known as *rapes*.

His wife Mabel having been killed in a feud in Normandy in 1082, Roger remarried to Adeliza de Puiset. Together they founded Shrewsbury Abbey, bringing monks from Sées to staff it, and the community, although not the magnificent red sandstone buildings, were complete by 1087. Roger also revived the monastery of St Milburga (an English royal saint) at Much Wenlock, and established a collegiate church at Quatford, also in Shropshire. His sense of piety was matched by his sense of place, and at Arundel he sponsored a priory dedicated to St Nicholas (the Normans' favourite saint).

Roger was the archetypical great lord of the Conquest, with nationwide power and cross-Channel authority. His adoption of local saints proved his determination to become an Englishman whilst remaining proud of his Norman inheritance. It seems that he was happy to remain in his adopted country when he died about 1093, at his Quatford castle: he was buried between the two altars of Shrewsbury Abbey rather than being returned to the duchy.

Hugh d'Avranches, earl of Chester (?–1101)

Hugh came from Danish stock in western Normandy, his grandfather Thurstan Goz having been a rebel against the young Duke William before the region was brought under ducal control in the 1050s. Hugh's father Richard made his peace with William, and Hugh inherited the county of Avranches at the western base of the Côtentin peninsula. He was a substantial supporter of the invasion and received William's gratitude by receiving lands in 20 counties. Gerbod, a Fleming, had been made responsible for Chester, but in 1071 he went back to Flanders and Hugh was awarded the territory and an earldom.

By this gift the Conqueror was recognising Hugh's talents as a warrior and his enormous energy in confronting the Welsh. With the help of his nephew Robert, he made inroads along the north coast, even reaching Anglesey. These territories were lost in 1093, when Hugh was in Normandy supporting William Rufus in the continuing disputes between the Conqueror's sons. On his return, Hugh reconquered the lands and punished the rebels by ravaging and mutilation, establishing a castle at Aberlleiniog on Anglesey. In 1098, Magnus Barelegs, king of Norway, raided the island and defeated Hugh.

Overall, though, Hugh was an immensely successful border baron. He was caricatured by the chronicler Orderic Vitalis as a man of gross appetites, both sexually, with many mistresses and bastard offspring, and at the table, becoming so fat that he could hardly walk. Although there may be truth in it, the story allows Orderic to contrast Hugh with his own earl, Roger of Shrewsbury, whose noble qualities embody Shropshire patriotism. Hugh was also known as *Lupus* (the Wolf) for his severity against the Welsh. For all his brutality Hugh seems to have been genuinely pious. When in 1092 he replaced the secular canons of St Werburgh's, Chester, with monks from Bec, he asked the saintly Archbishop Anselm to consecrate his new church (the present cathedral). The unlikely combination of these two men at the ceremony could have led to many jokes about the strange friendship between the Wolf and the Lamb.

Politics, strategy, the Church and administration

When William the Bastard, duke of Normandy, became William I, king of England, on Christmas Day 1066, he became the equal of his overlord, the king of France. In fact, potentially he was much more powerful than the Capetian monarch, because he had acquired the right to rule an ancient, powerful and wealthy kingdom whose resources far outmatched those of the Île-de-France. There were concomitant responsibilities of a military and strategic nature, of course, but the Anglo-Norman state threatened to be one of the most significant in north-western Europe. Although successive English kings were not always able to bring the full weight of their resources to bear on the Continent, the Norman and Angevin dynasties were dominant until the loss of Normandy (and much of the Angevin inheritance) under King John, in and after 1204. Possession of a large naval potential, together with ambitions in France, made this dominance possible.

Early attempts to influence events on the Continent were not propitious, however, as when William fitzOsbern sought to intervene in the succession dispute in Flanders. Supporting the young contender Arnulf, he was surprised, defeated and killed at the battle of Cassel in 1071. It may be that he had simply not taken enough men with him; a chronicler accused him of riding out 'as if to a tournament' rather than to war. This was a serious blow to King William, of course, who was deprived of one of the closest companions of his youth, and a very capable subordinate in whom he had placed great trust in establishing his rule in England.

England was only one realm in the British Isles and William had to contend with often aggressive neighbours. Scotland was an ancient monarchy, if much poorer and militarily weaker than its southern neighbour. The Scots had a tradition of raiding deep into northern England and much of the Borders was disputed territory for a century after the Conquest. Few English kings had dared campaign as far north as William did in 1072. Only the great tenth-century warrior-king Athelstan had been able to enforce his authority to the same extent, following the battle of Brunaburh in 937. It was not until 1157 that Henry II, heir to a vast Anglo-French empire, was able to force the return of Cumbria and Westmorland and recognition of English rule over Northumbria. King Malcolm led a major raid south in 1079, although William responded quickly with a counter-attack in the following year. In command was William's eldest son, Robert Curthose, who had been in rebellion against his father the previous year and now was in a brief moment of reconciliation. He was accompanied by that old campaigner his uncle, Earl Odo, as well as receiving support from Archbishop Lanfranc. The result was a successful ravaging of Lothian and renewed pledges of friendship from the King of Scots. This sufficed to keep Malcolm at bay for the rest of William's reign (although Malcolm resumed his attacks in the 1090s, seeking to exploit the strife between the Conqueror's sons).

The instability of the conquest years naturally led the Welsh princes to seek to exploit the situation, as had been the case before Harold's campaign of 1063. Defence soon turned to attack, however, as the invaders had a united realm and all the resources of rich lowland England behind them with which to wage war, while the Welsh political structure was fractured and their largely pastoral economy correspondingly poorer. William left the containment and subjection of the Welsh to capable subordinates. In the north, the

Fleming Gerbod, who had been given Chester, was soon replaced (by 1071) with Earl Hugh d'Avranches. His nephew, Robert of Rhuddlan, proved an aggressive ally and together they advanced the border across the River Dee, reaching as far as Conway. Domesday Book records that, for a payment of £40 to the king, Robert had been granted authority over all 'North Wales', although the boundaries of this territory are not defined. His acquisitions were held down by the castles of Rhuddlan and Deganwy, while Hugh built castles at Bangor, Caernarvon and (later) on Anglesey. So harsh was their rule, though, that the Welsh rebelled in 1093 and Robert was killed, so ending further expansion in the area for a while.

Against mid-Wales was set Roger de Montgomery's earldom based on Shrewsbury. He advanced towards the south-west, building castles at Caus and Montgomery (in southern Shropshire) before striking into the heart of Ceredigion. He established a castle at Cardigan on the west coast, and extended his authority southwards into Dyfed. He died in 1093, and his son Arnulf built a castle at Pembroke. This strong promontory site was both economically and strategically vital, and was never given up, even during the serious Welsh revolts of the twelfth century. This Montgomery advance met up with that of the lords of the southern Marches along the south coast. Initially, this was led by the ubiquitous William fitzOsbern, who constructed a strong castle on the cliff at Chepstow where the River Wye meets the Bristol Channel. The fine stone hall that he had built, effectively in the manner of a throne room, can still be seen today. He was literally irreplaceable though, and after his death William left it up to lesser marcher lords such as Lacy and Mortimer to continue the advance westward. In 1081, the king himself led an expedition to St David's during which he 'liberated many hundreds of men' (presumably slaves and hostages from earlier Welsh raids). With the help of its bishop he negotiated a truce with Rhys ap Tewdwr, ruler of Deheubarth, who agreed to pay £40 tribute, just as Robert of Rhuddlan had done in the north.

Western Wales was a natural jumping-off point for the conquest of Ireland. The Anglo-Saxon Chronicle suggests that 'King William would have conquered Ireland with his prudence and without any weapons, if he could have lived two years more.' Certainly, Arnulf de Montgomery formed a marriage alliance with the king of Munster as part of a similar policy. Ireland was to prove beyond the grasp of William and his heirs, however. It was not until two generations later, in 1169, that the ambitious earl of Pembroke was to begin an entrepreneurial invasion of Ireland (soon followed by a suspicious Henry II).

The reform and restructuring of the English Church

Although William had little opportunity to deal with ecclesiastical matters in the first years of the Conquest, in spring 1070 he convened a church council at Winchester, in the presence of the visiting papal legate, Ermenfrid. Since part of the justification for the invasion was the situation of the Church in England, with an excommunicate as archbishop of Canterbury – Stigand – and other alleged abuses, William needed to show that he took his responsibilities seriously. As a first step, only Stigand and two other bishops were deposed, while a third resigned, together with several abbots. The changes were not so much about putting English clergy out of office, but more to do with replacing the 'natural wastage' with men brought in from the Continent. Prime amongst them was the man who became archbishop of Canterbury – Lanfranc, abbot of William's personal foundation, the abbey of St Stephen's, Caen. He brought with him pupils and associates, such as his nephew Paul, who became abbot of St Albans. From Bec came Gundulf, who played a vital role as an administrator of the see of Canterbury before being appointed to Rochester, and was the architect of the Tower of London (and possibly Colchester Castle). Gilbert Crispin also came from Bec to become bishop of Westminster. Lanfranc held church councils

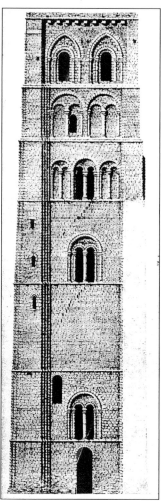

ABOVE LEFT The abbey church of St. Stephen's, Caen, founded by Duke William in penance for his marriage to Mathilda of Flanders. The classical Romanesque frontage of the building was imitated in the many new cathedrals of Norman England. (Ann Ronan Picture Library)

ABOVE RIGHT Canterbury Cathedral. The church was burnt down in 1067, at a time when rebellion was breaking out in England, but probably due to accident rather than guerrilla action. Its rebuilding was begun under Archbishop Lanfranc, who also ensured that the church was properly supported by its estates and provided due knight service. The building was completed by 1077 and is now represented by 'Lanfranc's Tower', shown here.

in 1072, 1075 and 1076, which sought to regularise ecclesiastical organisation and to reform the monasteries. He issued new 'Constitutions' to bring them into line with modern continental practice under the influence of a newly aggressive and reforming papacy. From William's point of view, what mattered was loyalty to his government, and so it is scarcely surprising that of the 18 appointments made during Lanfranc's episcopate (d. 1089), 16 were of Norman birth or training. Because senior ecclesiastics were essentially the top civil servants of his kingdom, William needed to make sure that they were committed to putting his policies into place.

The conflict between the sees of York and Canterbury illustrates the importance of this. Archbishop Ealdred, who crowned William and remained loyal, died a few days before the Danes sacked York in September 1069. In his place William chose Thomas, one of his

Securing the conquest 1072–1086

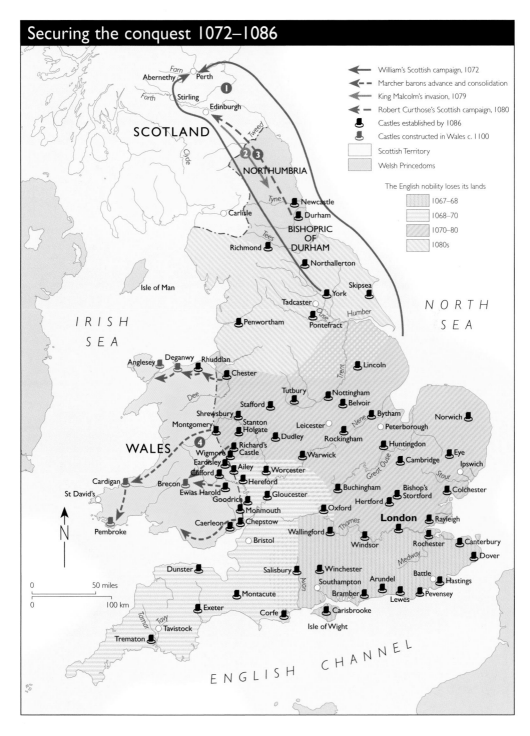

William's Scottish campaign, 1072

Marcher barons advance and consolidation

King Malcolm's invasion, 1079

Robert Curthose's Scottish campaign, 1080

Castles established by 1086

Castles constructed in Wales c. 1100

Scottish Territory

Welsh Princedoms

The English nobility loses its lands

1067–68

1068–70

1070–80

1080s

chaplains. Lanfranc was consecrated at Canterbury on 29 August 1070. Sometime in the autumn, Thomas came for his own consecration, but he refused Lanfranc's demands to offer submission. The problem

1   William's land and sea campaign of 1072; King of Scots submits.

2   1079 serious Scottish raid into Northumbria.

3   Robert Curthose leads reprisal campaign in 1080.

4   Marcher barons establish castles deep into Wales.

was what was called the 'primacy' issue. The see of Canterbury had been founded by St Augustine – 'Apostle to the English' – 500 years earlier and this, Lanfranc argued, meant

Domesday Book was a functional document, unlike the many highly decorated religious texts of the period. It was laid out according to a list of landowners in every shire, beginning with the king. Red titles were designed to draw the eye to each group of holdings, as were red lines through the letters. This was not a crossing-out, which was represented in the text by underlining (the reverse of modern practice).

that all other sees, including the archdiocese of York, were subject to his authority.

This was more than just a fine point of precedence. York was effectively the capital of a northern kingdom. Prior to the reign of Alfred the Great it had been part of Northumbria, and after it, for half a century, an independent Scandinavian statelet. Its absorption into the expanding kingdom of Wessex, which became a united England in the mid-tenth century, was not sufficiently thorough to prevent 'northern particularism'.

The stubborn resistance and repeated rebellions that had characterised the city and its shire until early 1070 meant that, only a few months later, William and his new archbishop were determined to dispel any remnants of separatism. After all, an independent archbishop of York might crown a king. Edgar aetheling remained a potential rival for over a decade and, as William was acutely aware, Ealdred of York had officiated at his own coronation. So Lanfranc's demands were influenced strongly by the requirements not just of politics but of military strategy. Why then was Thomas so obdurate? He had been the treasurer to Bayeux Cathedral, and a royal chaplain, making him a Norman courtier. The reason was that (like Becket a century later) a career-cleric felt a great responsibility to uphold the rights of the office to which he was appointed. Anything less would be betrayal of the church and its associated saint(s). In the end, the situation was resolved, but only after the case had been taken to the papal curia. Actually, the dispute rumbled on well into the twelfth century, but William had made his point. His writ ran everywhere in his kingdom.

There were other changes in the way the Church was arranged within the kingdom. Essentially, these had to do with the archaic English organisation that had grown up over centuries. The Conquest provided an opportunity to rationalise this structure and bring it in line with centres of population and, again, strategic need from the government's point of view. In some cases this meant relocating the minster (or cathedral), which was a bishop's most important church and the centre from which his diocese was run. So it was that the see of Lichfield was shifted to Chester, Sherborne to Salisbury, and Selsey to Chichester, Elmham to Thetford and finally to Norwich. Most dramatic of all was the move from Dorchester, on the Thames, to Lincoln, just south of the Humber and the independently minded northern shires. Apart, from Salisbury, where the combination of cathedral, castle and a new borough was effectively a 'new town' creation, all the moves located the bishop in a city that was the economic and strategic hub of the region that it dominated. This made sense from a military and administrative point of view as well as benefiting the Church.

Domesday Book: counting the cost of the Conquest

One aspect of William's character that was commented upon by contemporaries – especially his new English subjects – was how keen he was to know the resources of his realm. It was probably the military requirements of 1085, which so stretched William's resources in the face of imminent Danish invasion, that led to the great survey recorded in the volumes of Domesday Book. When the king kept his Christmas court at Gloucester, he:

had much thought and deep discussion with his council about this country – how it was occupied and with what sort of people. Then he sent his men all over England into every shire and had them find out how many hundred hides there were in the shire, or what land and cattle the king himself had in the country, or what dues he ought to have in twelve months from the shire.

William of St Calais, bishop of Durham (1081–96), seems to have supervised the whole exercise. The country was divided into circuits, composed of several shires, around which the teams of investigators rode. They were assisted by the sheriff of each county and, at local level, juries composed of men belonging to the *hundred* (named for representing units of 100 hides, the basic territorial unit of taxation). A description survives from the abbey of Ely, listing the questions that were asked (although these do not seem to have been standardised for every circuit):

Here follows the inquiry concerning the lands which the king's barons made according to the oath of the sheriff of the shire and of all the barons and their Frenchmen, and of the whole hundred court – the priest, reeves and six villeins from each village. They enquired what the manor was called; who held in the time of king Edward; who holds it now; how many hides there are; how many ploughs in [the lord's] demesne and how many belong to the men; how many villeins; how many cottars; how many slaves; how many freemen; how many sokemen; how much woodland; how much meadow; how much pasture; how many mills; how many fisheries; how much has been added to or taken away from the estate; what it used to be worth then; what it is worth now, and how much each freeman and sokeman had or has. All this to be recorded thrice: to wit, as it was in the time of King Edward, as it was when King William gave estate, and as it is now. And it was also noted whether more [taxes]

could be taken from the estate than is now taken. (Technical terms are explained in the glossary.)

As well as the yield that William expected to make, he was concerned to find out who actually held the land, and whether they had acquired it legally. The confusion, even

chaos, of the conquest years had led to the appropriation of estates by landlords, to which they may have had no genuine title. In the case of ecclesiastical lands, this pilfering was viewed as sacrilege. For the many dispossessed English landowning families there was probably no way back. They did not disappear altogether, but found themselves pushed down the social ladder while incomers, Normans, and men from other regions of Europe, reaped the benefits. Because an important aspect of landownership related to the provision of military service, William also needed to ascertain the extent of *knight service* available to him. Although Domesday Book is not arranged as a list of *fiefs* (as the military tenancies were called), by using it and other sources it is possible to estimate that William could call upon some 6,000 fully equipped warriors for his armies. Domesday does identify very clearly where the wealth and power lay in post-Conquest England. The king and his family owned about one-fifth of the lands surveyed, a dozen leading *tenants-in-chief* held about one-quarter, and the Church lands constituted a further quarter. This left only one-third in the hands of lesser landlords, and represented a much greater concentration of power in the hands of the new ruling elite than before 1066.

Understandably, perhaps, the English view of the survey – it was they who named it Domesday Book in the sense of it being like the account at the end of the world – was antagonistic.

[King William] had a record made of how much land his archbishops had, and his bishops and his abbots and his earls – and though I relate it at too great length – what or how much everybody who was occupying land in England, in land or cattle, and how much money was it worth. So very closely did he have it investigated,

The south-eastern corner of London's Roman walls served as the base for the royal castle in the city. Initially, a palisaded bank and ditch provided the fortified enclosure, later replaced with masonry, as shown here. (I.1570 The Conqueror's Castle. Impression of the Tower of London in 1080 by Ivan Lapper. copyright The Board of Trustees of the Armories)

that there was no single hide nor yard of land, nor indeed (it is a shame to relate but it seemed no shame to him to do) one ox nor one cow nor one pig which was there left out and not put down in his record, and all these records were brought to him afterwards.

Remarkably, this operation seems to have been completed in a year, including the work of compilation and writing-up. This activity took place at Winchester, the old 'capital' of Wessex, where the royal *scriptorium* (writing office) was still in place. Even more remarkable, according to manuscript scholars, the bulk of the work was done by just one scribe. The book itself survives in two volumes (although these were not bound until the seventeenth century). The larger, or 'Great Domesday', represents the final, much abbreviated version of the inquest's results. In contrast, 'Little Domesday', covering the eastern counties of Norfolk, Suffolk and Essex, contains much more detail, but is also more sketchily composed, with many erasures and uncorrected mistakes. A document known as

These three scenes from the Bayeux Tapestry represent the agricultural activities of the autumn. An ass draws a plough to create the furrows for sowing. Once the seeds have been sown by hand the soil is turned over to cover them by a harrow, in this case drawn by a horse. One of the changes brought about after 1066, was the use of equines rather than traditional oxen for such work. All that remains is for a boy to be detailed to scare off the birds with slingshot, in order for the crop to flourish. (Bayeux Tapestry. With special permission of the town of Bayeux)

the *Liber Exoniensis*, or Exon Domesday, relates to most (but not all) shires of the south-western circuit of the inquisitors. This provides even greater detail, and probably provides the material which was then summarised for the final compilation. Domesday Book, in its various forms, was used throughout the medieval period and, even later, for evidence in law cases, although the power of its name was often more significant than the information that it provided. Its creation, purpose and uses are still the subject of historical enquiry. The book remains an extraordinary survival and evidence of a period of transformation and of the obsession of one man: the Conqueror.

Three bishops: saint, architect and 'warrior'; and a queen

Saint Wulfstan of Worcester (c.1008–1095)

Wulfstan was remarkable as an Englishman who retained his bishopric, outlived the Conqueror, and oversaw changes for his diocese within the continuity that his long episcopacy allowed. His reputation as theologian, administrator and holy man (which led to his canonisation) is unparalleled. In 1062, Bishop Ealdred became archbishop of York, and the abbey's prior, Wulfstan, was elected to the see. Although representing the best of traditional Anglo-Saxon monasticism, he keenly supported the reforms introduced by Lanfranc, as archbishop of Canterbury, from 1070. He also supervised the rebuilding of the minster church in the grand *Romanesque* style found on the Continent and patronised by Edward the Confessor (although he is reported to have wept on viewing the destruction of the older, simple building).

As bishop, Wulfstan also held important responsibilities for the defence of the region, based upon the 300-hide territorial unit of Oswaldslow (capable of providing the cost of a warship and its fighting crew). Its leader was designated commander-in-chief of the bishop's forces. Wulfstan's utter loyalty to the new regime proved its value during the revolt of 1075, when he prevented the rebel Roger, earl of Hereford, from advancing westward, and in 1088, in support of the new king William II. He also coped with the predatory sheriff of Worcestershire, Urse d'Abitot (*shrievalty* 1069–1108), who had famously been cursed by Archbishop Ealdred for building a castle on the monastic cemetery.

Above all, Wulfstan was remembered for the simplicity of his life, recorded in hagiography by the monk Colman soon after his death and written-up by the Anglo-

Norman historian William of Malmesbury. The most famous anecdote to illustrate this was when Bishop Geoffrey of Coutances, notorious for his displays of wealth, urged Wulfstan to give up his lambskin cloak for one made of expensive cat fur like the Norman's. Wulfstan, apparently perplexed and not a little mischievous, replied that although he had often heard of the Lamb of God, he had never heard of the Cat of God.

Gundulf, bishop of Rochester (c.1024–1108)

A Norman, born near Rouen, Gundulf was educated at the cathedral school there and became a cleric. In 1057, following a vow made in peril of a storm at sea, he entered the monastery of Bec-Hellouin, founded by the former knight Herluin in 1039. The house's prior was the Italian Lanfranc, a former lawyer and monastic reformer whom Gundulf followed to St Stephen's, Caen, when it was established by Duke William in 1063. He went to England, where Lanfranc became archbishop of Canterbury in 1070, and Gundulf served as steward to the episcopal estates before being appointed bishop of Rochester in 1077. What made Gundulf special were his skills as an architect and builder. In addition to rebuilding Canterbury Cathedral, which had been destroyed by fire in 1067, he built many secular buildings, including castles.

Most notable was his supervision of the construction of the Tower of London – the White Tower – begun in 1077 and only half finished by the Conqueror's death. The building is typical of the *donjon*, or keep, type of construction of the era, but it is a very fine example. The fine ceremonial entrance (facing south) and the projecting apsidal

chapel (later copied at Colchester) make the Tower one of the most imposing fortresses of the time. Gundulf also constructed St Leonard's Tower at West Malling (for his own residence), began work on the castle at Rochester, and may have been involved in other fortification projects for the city of London, together with several smaller churches. Despite his continual involvement in building and administration, Gundulf did not neglect his episcopal duties and intervened to maintain standards in his monastic community as required. He had also formed a close friendship with Anselm, who had become a monk at Bec at about the same time as Gundulf and proved himself one of the most sensitive theologians of his age. This showed that the practical man

These two scenes from the Bayeux Tapestry portray the work's patron: Odo, bishop of Bayeux and earl of Kent. His twin titles describe his dual role. Not all bishops were as bellicose as Odo, and the reforming papacy of the late eleventh century was strongly against such behaviour. The scene (above) showing the fighting at Hastings may exaggerate Odo's role to flatter him; while his blessing of the meal before the battle (right), although conventional, is based upon the Last Supper, with the bishop sitting in the place of Christ! There was no doubting Odo's value to his half-brother, though, as viceroy, justiciar, administrator, wealthy cleric and propagandist for the Norman regime. (Bayeux Tapestry. With special permission of the town of Bayeux.)

could also grasp abstract ideas. When Anselm was made archbishop of Canterbury in 1089, the relationship continued, and it was the archbishop who attended Gundulf in his last illness and conducted his burial service.

Odo, bishop of Bayeux and earl of Kent (c.1030 or 1035–1097)

In around 1030, Duke Robert of Normandy married-off Herlève, William's mother, to Herluin de Conteville, and she soon produced two half-brothers to the bastard duke. Odo was the elder, born soon after the marriage and made bishop of Bayeux in 1049 (although well under canonical age). He proved himself an invaluable support to Duke William, until they fell out in 1082, for reasons which are unclear, and he was imprisoned on the king's orders.

Odo has a popular reputation as a fighting bishop, which might make his inclusion in a non-military group seem perverse, but his main contribution to the Conquest was as an administrator and *justiciar* for his brother's regime. His role at Hastings, like that of another active bishop, Geoffrey of Coutances, was to 'give aid by their prayers' at the rear. The 'mace' which he is depicted carrying on the Bayeux Tapestry is not a weapon but a baton of command, such as Duke William is also shown wielding. The Tapestry was constructed on Odo's orders, so it may well exaggerate his part at Hastings, but it also shows him performing the more conventional task of blessing a meal.

Odo has also been given a bad reputation by twelfth-century Anglo-Norman historians, who accuse him of the acquisition of ecclesiastical estates. Yet the abbeys of

Gundulf, bishop of Rochester, was commissioned as architect of a central *donjon* (keep) of London's royal fortress. This was a palace built in tower form with carefully arranged rooms for ceremonial purposes. Only completed after King William's death, the 'White Tower' became the representation of royal government for centuries. This view shows the apsidal projection of the chapel of St John, situated on the first floor. (Spectrum Colour Library)

St Augustine's, Canterbury, and St Albans, and the bishopric of Rochester all acknowledged his protection and support. He was an immensely wealthy lord, with lands worth £3,000 according to Domesday Book. These lay largely in Kent, where he was earl, but also in Buckinghamshire, Hertfordshire and Lincolnshire (essentially following the stages of the campaigns of the Conquest). He seems to have acted in a vice-regal role on many occasions and took part in the northern campaign with Robert Curthose in 1080. Released from prison in 1088 by William's death-bed pardon, Odo supported Robert's rebellion against William Rufus in the same year. When this failed, the bishop withdrew increasingly to Bayeux. In fact, he had not neglected his diocese over the conquest years, having been there often before 1082, especially for the consecration of his grand new cathedral in 1077 (when the Tapestry may first have been displayed).

For the next decade, Odo was occupied in Normandy, encouraging Duke Robert to exercise more than lax control over his rebellious vassals. Perhaps frustrated by his waning influence, and although in his 60s, Odo set out to join the First Crusade. While visiting Norman Sicily in January 1097, he died of a virulent but unknown disease and was buried in the cathedral at Palermo.

Queen Edith, wife of Edward the Confessor (?–1075)

The third child and eldest daughter of Earl Godwine, Edith was married to King Edward in 1045 in an attempt to ensure her family's succession to the kingdom. That she bore the king no children was probably due to infertility, although after Edward's canonisation this was represented as a celibate marriage. It may have been the lack of an heir that caused Edward to repudiate her during the exile of her father and brothers in 1051. She lost her lands, and was reportedly sent to the nunnery at Wherwell in humiliating circumstances, accompanied by only one female attendant. When her father and brothers returned the following summer, she was reinstated.

Edith seems to have favoured Tostig, even to the extent of having some of his Northumbrian opponents murdered at her command. This act, and other persecutions by her brother, prompted a northern rebellion which saw him exiled to Flanders. Harold was left clear to claim the throne on Edward's death. Edith retired to Winchester, and may have connived with Tostig in his attempt to return. After the battle of Hastings she handed the city over to William's troops and was allowed to remain in residence. It may also have been her intervention that prevented King William from acting more harshly against the south-western rebels in 1067, since the city of Exeter was in her *dower*. Unlike her mother, Gytha, she does not seem to have contemplated rebellion, nor to have supported her nephews (Harold's sons) in their attacks on the region. She favoured the nunnery of Wilton, near Salisbury, and may have spent her later years there, although she died at Winchester in December 1075.

Edith sponsored a biography (effectively a saint's life) of her husband, which provides some of the details of her relationship with the king and her family. The events of 1066 were truly traumatic for the queen. Her four remaining brothers were killed and her dynasty's pretensions smashed by William's successful conquest. The tone of Edward's *vita*, written contemporaneously, changes to reflect these momentous events, but the queen's own feelings are nowhere represented and can only be guessed at.

The Conqueror's reign

Unlike modern conflicts between two powers, which are mostly resolved by a treaty and some return to the status quo (although borders may be adjusted), the Norman Conquest saw the end of the native royal line and a replacement of the nobility by outsiders. The war of conquest was effectively over by the end of 1071, although the Scottish campaign of the following year was important in assuring, at least temporarily, the northern borders against attack. What the meeting at Abernethy was really about, though, was making the King of Scots recognise the legitimacy of William's rule. After all, Malcolm had sheltered the aetheling Edgar since 1068, and supported the young prince's campaigns around York. Malcolm's submission led Edgar to flee to Flanders, not returning until 1074, when a shipwreck meant that he regained Scotland only with difficulty. At some time before then Malcolm had married Edgar's sister Margaret, apparently against the Englishman's wishes – but there was little that a landless exile could do about it. So Edgar submitted to William, and was received into his court, effectively as a royal hostage. He is described as receiving unspecified honours, but there is no record of the return of the lands which he had been granted before his rebellion.

Edgar is recorded as being 14 in 1066, the same age as William's eldest son, Robert, and they seem to have struck up a close friendship. Robert became dissatisfied with his father's reluctance to delegate any responsibility to him, and rebelled on several occasions. Although Edgar did not join him, he did leave England in 1086, apparently unhappy at his low status, and travelled to southern Italy. He returned to play a part in the succession dispute following the Conqueror's death in 1087, only to find his companion Robert denied the throne by William Rufus. In exile again by 1091, Edgar is often described as having led an English fleet on the First Crusade (1096–99). This is due to a confusion by a twelfth-century chronicler. In fact, Edgar did not visit the Holy Land until 1102. He was back in the West in 1106, again supporting Robert against Henry I. Both were captured at the battle of Tinchebrai in 1106. While Robert was imprisoned by his vengeful brother until his death in 1136, Edgar was allowed to retire to his estates. Where these were is uncertain, but they may have been in Normandy, and he is believed to have died peacefully around 1125.

So William faced no real threat from the English royal line after 1072. Yet the king had pressing military obligations in France. So it is not surprising that he returned to Normandy in 1073 to contest Maine with Fulk, count of Anjou. In another swift campaign he recovered the county, taking Le Mans at the end of March. Meanwhile, Philip I, King of France, who had been under the guardianship of William's father-in-law until 1067, on assuming his majority had begun to act against the king-duke. In 1074, he apparently offered the castle of Montreuil-sur-Mer, strategically placed just south of Boulogne, to Edgar aetheling, as a base from which to attack William – although, as we have seen, the Englishman preferred to be reconciled with the king. Philip, allied with Fulk of Anjou, did manage to stir up trouble on William's western border in Brittany. Several Breton lords contested the Norman supremacy, among them Ralph de Gael, whose father had served King Edward, and who held extensive lands in England also.

In 1075, a potentially serious rebellion broke out in England. This seems to have been initiated by Ralph, who was marrying the daughter of Roger de Breteuil, earl of Hereford (and William fitzOsbern's second son). Indeed, the Anglo-Saxon Chronicle asserts that the plot was hatched at the wedding feast, held at Exning, near Newmarket. The rebels also brought in Waltheof, earl of Huntingdon, the only surviving English noble of high rank in the kingdom. It is his involvement that links the revolt to the Conquest, for otherwise it was really part of a wider conflict being levied by William's opponents in France. Also, the rebellion was so ineptly managed that the king's deputies in England had no difficulty suppressing it without his presence. Indeed, Archbishop Lanfranc wrote to William urging him to concentrate on his continental opponents. From a military point of view, what makes the suppression of the rebellion interesting is the way that castles played a crucial role. Even the Anglo-Saxon Chronicle, which represents the fortifications as a foreign intrusion, recognised this. Explaining

the rebels' lack of success, it records: 'the castle men who were in England and also the local people came against them and prevented them from doing anything'. The strategic dispositions of the rebels hardly helped their cause, as they were unable to unite their forces. Roger, based on the Welsh borders, was held at bay by Wulfstan, bishop of Worcester, and Aethelwig, abbot of Evesham (both native Englishmen), supported by the Norman lords of the western midlands. Ralph was unable to escape from Norfolk because Odo of Bayeux, earl of Kent, and other lords blocked his path. The rebels were forced to flee abroad.

In 1078, Robert, the Conqueror's eldest son, rebelled, angry that his father would not delegate power to him. Philip, king of France, was happy to stir the pot and entrusted Robert with the castle of Gerberoi, on the borders of Normandy. When William attacked the place, he was defeated in battle, and may even have been unhorsed by his son, as this picture shows. The scene is also evocative of castle warfare: dominated by the need for sieges, with cavalry operating around the fortifications. (Christa Hook)

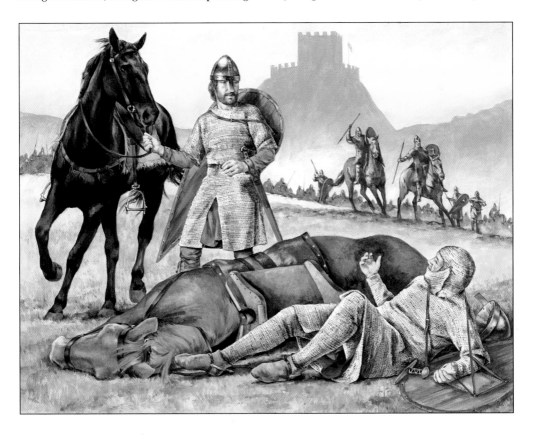

The only remaining threat was posed by a Danish fleet, under its new king, Cnut, who may have been in contact with Ralph. The 200 ships arrived too late to play any part in the fighting, so the Danes contented themselves with raiding northwards up the east coast, eventually reaching York and sacking St Peter's before sailing away to escape retribution. William's triumph had been to ensure the safety of his realm, while he himself was occupied elsewhere. The rebels lost their estates, but not their lives – except, that is, for Earl Waltheof, who was executed at Winchester in May 1076. Historians have commented on William's harshness in this case, in contrast with his usual clemency, but the reason may have to do with the law. Was it that Waltheof, as an Englishman, suffered his nation's punishment for treason, while the French and Bretons paid a lighter price? Or it may be that William had lost patience with a man whom he had already pardoned for rebellion. Clearly, no Englishman of high birth was any longer acceptable in a position of authority, only a decade after the invasion.

William's Breton expedition in 1077 did not go according to plan. He was defeated outside Dol; it was the first time he had suffered a reverse in over 20 years. This, together with his son Robert's rebellion in 1078, left him looking vulnerable in his continental possessions. William was defeated again, outside the castle of Gerberoi (in the lands known as the Vexin, lying across the Seine between the French king's territory and Normandy). A chronicle account depicts Robert unhorsing his father in a joust, although this may be romantic elaboration. In England, however, the reverse was the case. A Scottish invasion – or glorified raid – in 1079 was punished the following year by an expedition led by Robert (by now restored to favour). His forces ravaged Lothian, advancing as far north as Falkirk and enforcing upon Malcolm the provisions of the 1072 submission.

In fact, the last threat to William's regime came from England's oldest enemy: the Danes. In 1074, the king had written to Lanfranc insisting that the eastern shires be prepared for seaborne attack. When he heard of another threatened invasion in 1085, William required even more desperate measures. According to the Anglo-Saxon Chronicle:

William ... who was then in Normandy ... went to England with a larger force of mounted men and foot-soldiers from France and Brittany than had ever come to this country, so that people wondered how they could all be supported. And the king had the army dispersed all over the country among his men, and they provisioned them each according in proportion to his land. And the people had much oppression that year, and the king had the land near the sea laid waste, so that if his enemies landed, they should have nothing to seize on so quickly.

In the event, Cnut was prevented from setting out by domestic political problems. The taxes that he raised to pay for the expedition were resisted, and when he tried again the next year he was murdered and the invasion plan collapsed. So, as it turned out, William's drastic preparations proved unnecessary. Yet, even after two decades as king, he was acutely aware of the vulnerability of his realm to a large seaborne invasion. It was the events of that year that led to the creation of Domesday Book, one of the most important documents of English history. A major part of the purpose of the survey was to assess what tax revenue was available to the Crown for its vital task of securing the kingdom from attack. Through the survey, William strengthened his power to defend the measure of security that he had already achieved for the kingdom, despite rebellions and incursions after his campaigns of conquest from 1066 to 1072.

The English experience: law, culture and society

The regulation of warfare

It is to be expected that a military conquest will have grave implications for the civilian population of any country. This was true in the mid-eleventh century, but the limited scale of military activity meant that the impact was not as pervasive as in modern warfare. Rather it was localised and short-term. This is not to say that war brought no problems to peasants or townsmen and their families, or to the celibate monks and nuns whose abbeys were repositories of enormous wealth. In fact, any historian relying upon the monastic chroniclers for evidence could be misled by their accounts of brutality and theft directed at vulnerable servants of God. Yet it was not in the long-term interests of rulers to have either productive peasants or ecclesiastical sites damaged by the ravages of war. It was, of course, in the short-term interests of their campaigning soldiery to take advantage of a profitable situation where they could. Nor should any difference in attitude be assumed between the knights and their less well-off followers; each could be equally rapacious. Yet there were constraints placed upon warfare for precisely this reason. The Church had been preaching a code aimed at restricting warfare for over half a century, known as the Peace and Truce of God. The former meant that certain individuals were to be exempt from abuse in warfare: women and children, clerics, merchants and so on; the latter referred to the attempt to keep holy days (essentially Friday through Monday) free from conflict. Understandably, these approaches met with limited success, although rulers were also keen to encourage them as it helped to prevent local 'private' wars, or feuds, in their territories. Duke William had proved himself enthusiastic for their promulgation, especially just before his great expedition overseas. He also instituted a penitential code in his new kingdom, designed both to punish his warriors for the sins they necessarily incurred in warfare and to cleanse them from those sins. Its institution is associated with the arrival of the papal legate in 1070, and its 11 clauses provide important insights into how contemporaries dealt with the violence and rapine associated with William's campaigns.

Several deal with Hastings, requiring a year's (unspecified) penance for every person killed by a warrior 'in the great battle', with shorter periods if he were unsure whether he actually killed anyone with a blow, or, like an archer, inflicted unknown wounds from a distance. Clerics who fought, or who were armed for fighting, were also penalised (although there is no record of what Bishop Odo thought of this). The text makes a distinction between the period before William's consecration and afterwards. So, before the end of 1066, a soldier fighting in what was called the 'public war', that is legitimately serving the Conqueror, was asked to do a year's penance for killing anyone whilst in search of legitimate supplies for the army. If this was deemed looting, however, the penance was three times as heavy. Killing in a similar situation, after William was crowned, was deemed murder of the king's subject, unless that person was actively in arms against the king. Inner motivation was also considered important. Killing for personal gain was considered murder, although if it was done in 'public war' a three-year penance was substituted. Rape was also considered a matter for penance, with the punishment assessed depending upon the country of the perpetrator. Another concomitant of warfare, although deeply frowned upon as sacrilegious, was attacks on and theft from churches. Bishops were directed to try to restore the property of looted churches, or to give it to another church if the original provenance could not be found.

Establishing the law

The penitential code shows that contemporaries were aware of the cruelty and unregulated violence generated in a country during wartime. There were established law codes, aiming to control such behaviour, although it might not always have been possible to enforce them in troubled times. There was also the problem of likely clashes between the incomers – all called 'French' in legal documents – and the native English population. The 'Ten Articles of William the Conqueror', an unofficial compilation of laws attributed to the king in the early twelfth century, show what concerned the new ruler. He required an oath of loyalty from every freeman (no. 2), and a promise to defend the kingdom, which we know was enforced in 1085 as the threat of a Danish invasion loomed. In return, William promised to keep the law of King Edward 'in respect of their lands and possessions, with the addition of those decrees which I have ordained for the welfare of the English people' (no. 7). The possibility of the murder of a new landlord by a resentful Englishman is covered, together with the responsibility first for his lord and then the wider community to pay compensation for such an act (no. 3). Trial by battle was introduced as a way of deciding innocence in cases of murder, robbery, perjury or theft, although an Englishman unused to this novelty could elect for the ancient ordeal of the hot iron

instead (no. 6). In a combination of English and Norman customs William established a system of *frankpledge*, which is to say surety groups established at local level to ensure that wrong-doers were handed over to the proper authorities for judgement (no. 8). All these laws provided some kind of security for those considered 'free' men and women, in

This reconstruction of a typical English *burh* gives some idea of the scale of urban development before the Conquest. In the central foreground old Roman walls have been used, while elsewhere an earth and timber ditch-and-bank forms the defences. The site is somewhat reminiscent of Wareham, Dorset, or Wallingford. (Gerry Embleton)

other words those entitled to justice. There was a substantial group in English society in 1066 who were 'unfree' though: the slave population. Article Nine forbade the selling of one by another outside the country, on payment of a fine; and one impact of the Norman Conquest was to be the steep reduction in slave-holding.

The population

The impact of the wars on the towns of England also needs consideration. There were over 100,000 burgesses in the kingdom in 1086, perhaps a fifth of them in London alone, which may have grown dramatically since 1066. By contrast the ancient city of

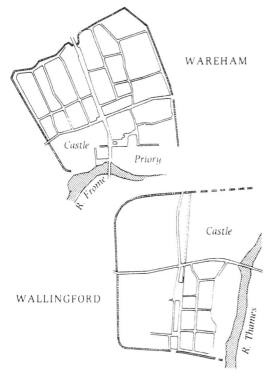

WAREHAM

Castle

Priory

R. Frome

Castle

WALLINGFORD

R. Thames

The English *burhs* of Wareham and Wallingford (also in the photograph) show the impact of the Conquest upon the kingdom's fortifications. Both stand on strategic river sites: Wareham near the coast and the great expanse of Poole harbour, Wallingford at a crucial crossing of the Thames. The Normans placed castles within them, occupying almost a quarter of the site, and reinforced the defences with a raised tower and bailey walls. This enormously strengthened royal power, which was not seriously challenged for two generations. (Above, University of Cambridge Collection of Air Photos)

Winchester had a population of about 5,000, York and the important entrepôt of Bristol only about 4,000, with other sites barely reaching 2,000. The importance of London, visible at least since King Alfred's time, had been increased by King Edward's development of Westminster. Apart from the burning of the south-bank enclave of Southwark, the city seems to have been little damaged in 1066. Very early in his reign, possibly in 1067, William recognised London's status as a borough, and the wording of the text, written in English, shows how keen he was to have the citizens on his side:

William the king greets William, bishop of London, and Gosfrith the portreeve, and all the burgesses of London friendly. I give you to know that I will be worthy of all the laws you were worthy of in the time of King Edward. And I will that every child shall be his father's heir after his father's day. And I will not suffer any man to do you wrong. God preserve you.

The situation at York, so often rebellious from 1068 to 1070, must have been very different. The destruction of its cathedral, St Peter's, in September 1069 must represent much wider destruction. It is difficult to believe that the population can have escaped the ravages of war as the ownership of the place changed hands so frequently. Then there was the deliberate ravaging of its shire in 1069–70, which, even if the chronicler exaggerates with his '100,000' death toll, must have been devastating for the region. The damage is still visible in Domesday Book, after a decade and a half of peace. The destruction was not restricted to Yorkshire, but was inflicted in a broad swathe across the northern shires, the west Midlands and the Welsh border.

The greatest impact on non-combatants in the wider population might be termed a silent revolution. This was the gradual replacement of the Anglo-Danish aristocracy and its retainers, which had been in place for over half a century, by Norman and other continental landlords. This took place earliest in the south-eastern corner of the kingdom (1067–68), spreading to the south-west and the southern Marches (1068–70). The events of 1069–70 caused this development in a region devastated in 1070–71, while East Anglia was more slowly colonised over the 1070s. As to the lands 'north of Humber', they did not really come into the invaders' possession until the 1080s. (See Map on p. 67) North of that, Northumberland proper and Cumbria were disputed lands with the Scots, and the bishopric of Durham was an independent

territory (palatinate), although this did not mean that these regions escaped a change in ownership. The non-combatant population of England could not help but be affected by the campaigns of the Conquest but, although some experienced all the horrors of war, for most the impact was slow and consisted of deep-rooted social change rather than fire and the sword.

The Conquest through English eyes

One of the most important aspects of English culture in the eleventh century was the extent to which its vernacular tongue was in use. In the rest of Europe where the Latin Church held sway, its sacred language was also that of government. In England, kings issued charters and writs – a brief instruction, usually to a sheriff, to carry out a particular act at the king's will – in English. This meant that a *ceorl*, or peasant, could quite literally converse with the king, or make his case in court in front of the justice and his peers. In addition, there was a wealth of literary texts in English, much of it ecclesiastical and theological, but it also included a great deal of poetry, rhymes, riddles and sayings that reflected popular culture. Above all, there was a chronicle tradition in the form of annals (accounts of each year) initiated by Alfred the Great in the 890s. The Anglo-Saxon Chronicles, as they should properly be called because several versions survive, written in different parts of the country and with differing political perspectives, record the views of a defeated people. The impact of the Conquest on the religious houses that sponsored the history's creation can be seen in the disappearance of all but the Peterborough version after 1080, which itself lasted until 1154.

The Chronicles provide nothing other than brief notices for the battle of Hastings although they do say more about the immediate impact of the Conquest. According to the 'D' version, before William's coronation at Westminster:

RIGHT The little town of Eye, in Norfolk, still shows strongly the original Norman layout. It was part of William Malet's fief, inherited by Robert after his father's death in the Fenland campaign of 1071. At the top of the picture, the church stands east of the castle motte. The construction of new houses in the 1980s show clearly the line of the original bailey. The burgesses' houses followed the line of the castle walls, linked by the encircling road, and the old market place was probably on the site of the modern car-park! (Suffolk Record Office)

BELOW King William I's royal seal, attached to documents to authorise them. The obverse shows him as *Dux Normannorum*, armed and mounted as a knight. On the reverse he is shown seated in majesty (on a throne holding a sword in his right hand and the orb in his left), as king of England. The distinction suggests that he saw himself as the ruler of separate territories, and this is how he disposed of them on his death, his son Robert becoming duke and William II 'Rufus', king. (Ann Ronan Picture Library)

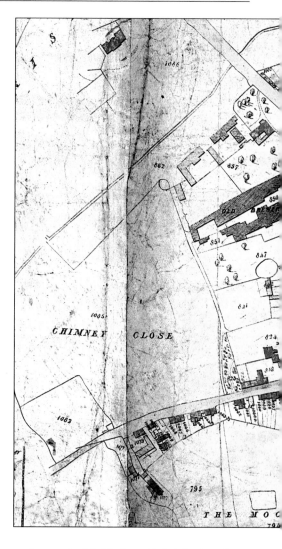

he promised Ealdred on Christ's book and swore moreover (before Ealdred would place the crown upon his head) that he would rule all this people as well as the best of the kings before him, if they would be loyal to him. All the same he laid taxes on people very severely, and then went in spring overseas to Normandy, and took with him [the principal magnates] ... and many other good men from England. And bishop Odo and earl William stayed behind and built castles far and wide throughout this country and distressed the wretched folk, and always after that it grew much worse. May the end be good when God wills it!

For the year 1087, the annal is very long and almost entirely devoted to an assessment

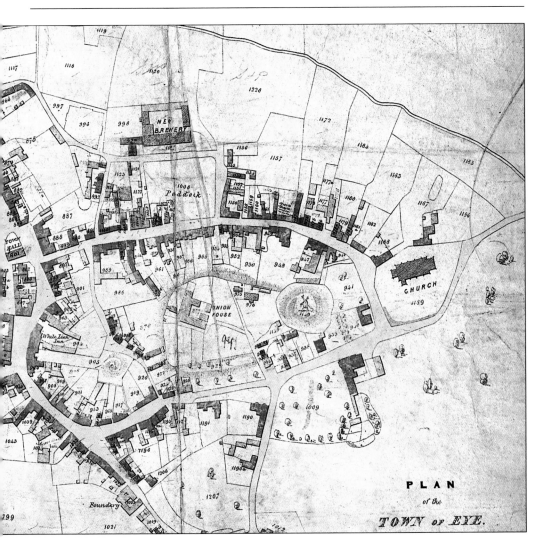

PLAN
of the
TOWN OF EYE.

of King William and his rule. Although he is praised for supporting the Church, and especially monks (which suited the writer of course, as he was one), William is criticised for his heavy taxes and for extracting harsh terms from his vassals.

The king and his chief men loved gain much and over-much – gold and silver – and did not care how sinfully it was obtained provided it came to them. The king sold his land on very hard terms – as hard as he could. Then came somebody else and offered more than the other had given, and the king let it go to the man who had offered more. Then came a third, and offered still, and the king gave into the hands of the man who offered him most of all, and did not care how sinfully the reeves had got it from poor men, nor how many unlawful things they did. But the more just laws were talked about, the more unlawful things were done. They imposed just tolls and did many injustices which are hard to reckon up.

The chronicler writes about William's virtues too, recognising that his strong rule had brought peace and security.

This King William of whom we speak was a very wise man, and very powerful and more worshipful and stronger than any predecessor of his had been. He was gentle to the good men who loved God and stern beyond all measure to those people who resisted his will … Also he was very

dignified: three times every year he wore his crown, as often as he was in England. At Easter he wore it at Winchester, at Whitsuntide at Westminster, and at Christmas at Gloucester, and then there were with him all the powerful men over all England, archbishops and bishops, abbots and earls, thegns and knights. Also, he was a very stern and violent man, so that no one dared do anything contrary to his will. He had earls in fetters, who acted against his will. He expelled bishops from their sees, abbots from their abbacies, and put thegns in prison, and finally did not spare his own brother, who was called Odo ...

Finally, the writer breaks into verse to vent his feelings. Again he criticises William for his greed, and for protecting game, reserving hunting rights (as he did in the New Forest) with blinding or mutilation as a punishment for poaching. A single phrase encompasses the monk's response, which must have struck a chord with so many of the English under Norman rule: 'He had castles built/ and poor men hard oppressed'.

English literary culture, such as is represented here by the Chronicle, was not

LEFT Scheme of a Norman castle based on Castle Hedingham, Essex, showing the enclosed fortified courtyard leading, via drawbridge and gateway, to fortified castle on raised mound, all surrounded by defensive moat. (Ann Ronan Picture Library)

ABOVE King William's reputation long out-lived his reign. IN the mid twelfth century, Norman barons, anxious to assert their traditional rights against the Angevin Henry II, stressed their role in his conquest. In this thirteenth-century representation William is shown (as on his seal) armed

destroyed by the Conquest. However, English was replaced as the language of government by Latin, and in law by Latin and French. Anyone who wished to play a part in secular or ecclesiastical politics needed to speak French, which became the language of the court. Orderic Vitalis provides a rosier picture of both the language divide and William's intentions:

The king's passion for justice dominated the kingdom, encouraging others to follow his example. He struggled to learn some of the English language, so that he could understand the pleas of the conquered people without an interpreter, and benevolently pronounced fair judgements for each one as justice required. But advancing age prevented him from acquiring such learning, and the distractions of his many duties forced him to give his attention to other things.

While it is true that English was submerged for a time, it did not actually take three centuries – until the golden age of Chaucer and Henry V's deliberate act of policy – to revive. By c.1200, a Worcestershire cleric called Layamon was writing a history of King Arthur in English. Although the story related to a native legend, it was part of French chivalric culture. This serves to make the work representative of the synthesis of nations, languages and cultures that the Conquest had brought about.

King William's interest in ecclesiastical reform did not prevent him being accused of oppressing the Church as his youngest son, Henry I (1100–1135) is here represented being accused in a dream. Below is shown the disaster of the White Ship, in which Henry's heir was drowned, precipitating two decades of civil war and the end of the Norman dynasty. (Worcester Chronicle c.1140, Edimedia)

Glossary

aetheling: a prince of the English line with a claim to the throne.

beserker: a viking warrior, based entirely on legend, who supposedly went into a battle rage.

burh: English communal fortification devised to defeat the vikings, used both defensively and offensively to reconquer territory.

canonisation: official recognition by the Pope that an individual's acts were worthy of their being declared a saint.

castellan: authorised governor of a castle; he could be a great lord or a more subordinate figure.

castellany: lands associated with the upkeep and garrisoning of a castle.

ceorl: English term for a non-noble individual, who could be a peasant or someone much richer, such as a merchant.

chevalier: French word meaning a rider but implying warrior status: a knight.

cottar: technical term for a peasant found in Domesday Book.

Danegeld: term used for payments made to buy protection from viking raids and Danish invasion.

Danelaw: territories north of the Thames and east of Watling Street (modern A5) which had been under Danish rule in the tenth century and retained distinctive practices as regards law and nomenclature.

donjon: French word for the tall central tower (keep) of a castle, symbolising authority and derived from the Latin term *dominium*.

dower: a widow's property or landholdings.

dux Anglorum: 'commander-in-chief of the English', a term used to describe Harold Godwineson. The English word duke conveys the idea of non-royal authority.

earl: a great landowner with responsibility for a collection of shires, e.g. Wessex.

Fabian tactics: avoiding battle against an enemy, hoping to wear him down by attrition.

fealty: personal oath of loyalty sworn by a vassal to his lord.

The Fens (fenland): a low-lying area of East Anglia which was regularly inundated and so a good base for vikings and English rebels.

fief: a military tenancy which was rewarded with a gift of land or monetary support.

frankpledge: communal surety group designed to keep the peace.

fyrd: English word for an army; a general levy of troops from a shire.

to harry: to devastate the lands of rebels or opponents in war.

hauberk: knee-length mail shirt worn as armour by fully equipped warriors.

heregeld: army tax raised specifically under the Danish kings and abandoned by King Edward in 1051; from **here:** English word for an army.

hide: a land valuation equivalent to the annual production of one peasant family, used by governments to assess obligations for taxation and military service.

hundred: territorial unit nominally of 100 hides, and a sub-division of a shire, with its own law court and responsibilities for maintaining peace.

huscarl: (housecarl) a member of the close military following of an Anglo-Danish lord, he could live in the household (hearth-troop) or be a landed follower.

justiciar: chief justice of the kingdom, subordinate only to the king in legal matters.

knight: derived from the English word *cnicht*, meaning retainer or follower; in post-Conquest England it came to mean a fully equipped warrior and member of a social elite.

knight service: the military obligation of an individual, community or institution.

The Marches: Welsh border, from the French for a war frontier; **Marcher lord**.

pallium: ceremonial stole worn by the archbishop of Canterbury to symbolise his legitimate authority conferred by the Pope.

papal curia: the Pope's court, today known as the Vatican.

the rapes: territorial units grouped along the south coast and used to support *castellanies*, such as Arundel, in defence of the region.

reeve: English term meaning a servant who administered territory or a community (shire reeve = sheriff).

Romanesque: a style of architecture popular in eleventh-century Europe, usually portrayed by its use of round archways in great aisled churches.

saga(s): Scandinavian and Icelandic poems about legendary heroic deeds; mostly written down in the thirteenth century; they should be used as evidence for earlier events only with caution.

scriptorium: the writing office of the king or, usually, ecclesiastical institution, which produced the documents of government and administration.

sheriff: royal official responsible for the administration of a shire.

shield-wall: poetic description of the Anglo-Danish battle-line used to describe men fighting on foot, in both close and looser order.

shire: English word for a sub-division of the kingdom, later called a county.

shrievalty: a sheriff's term of office.

silvaticus: Latin term meaning woodsman; a rebel or outlaw forced to live in the forests and using them as a base to raid new Norman territories.

sokeman: technical term found in Domesday Book for a non-noble freeman who had rights to justice.

staller: English term for a royal household officer originally associated with management of horses, but by the eleventh century with broader responsibilities.

steppe nomads: members of horse-based cultures living on the grasslands of Asia and Eurasia whose main weapon was the horse-archer; difficult enemies for the armies of more settled cultures.

tenant-in-chief: land-holding vassal who held directly of the king; a great lord.

thegn: English term for a fully equipped warrior, usually associated with the ownership of at least five hides of land.

vassal: the sworn follower of a lord, providing military service in return for lands.

villein: technical term for a peasant found in Domesday Book.

vita: Latin for 'life', the term used for a saint's biography.

Further reading

Barlow, F., *Edward the Confessor*, 1970
Barlow, F., ed., *The Life of King Edward who Lies at Westminster*, 1992
Bates, D., *Normandy before 1066*, 1982
Bates, D., *William the Conqueror*, 2000
Beeler, J., *Warfare in England 1066–1189*, 1966
Bradbury, J., *The Battle of Hastings*, 1998
Brown, R.A., *The Normans and the Norman Conquest*, 1969
Brown, R.A., *Documents of the Norman Conquest*, 1994
Brown, R.A., et al., ed., *Anglo-Norman Studies: Proceedings of the Battle Conference*, annual 1979 on
Campbell, J., *The Anglo-Saxons*, 1982
Chibnall, M., ed., *The Ecclesiastical History of Orderic Vitalis*, 6 vols., 1969–80
Davis, R.H.C., and Chibnall, M., eds., *The Gesta Guillelmi of William of Poitiers*, 1998
Davis, R.H.C., ed., *The Carmen de Hastingae Proelio*, 1998
De Vries, K., *The Norwegian Invasion of 1066*, 1999
Douglas, D.C., *William the Conqueror*, 1964
Gibson, M., *Lanfranc of Bec*, 1978
Grape, W., *The Bayeux Tapestry: Monument to a Norman Triumph*, 1994
Gravett, C., *Hastings 1066*, 1992
Gravett, C., *Norman Knight*, 1993
Griffith, P., *The Viking Art of War*, 1995
Hallam, E.M., *Domesday Book through Nine Centuries*, 1986
Harrison, M., *Anglo-Saxon Thegn 449–1066*, 1993
Hayward Gallery exhibition catalogue *English Romanesque Art 1066–1200*, 1984
Higham, N.J., *The Death of Anglo-Saxon England*, 1997
Hollister, C.W., *Anglo-Saxon Military Institutions on the Eve of the Norman Conquest*, 1962

Hollister, C.W., *The Military Organization of Anglo-Norman England*, 1965
Hooper, N., and Bennett, M., *Cambridge Atlas of Warfare: the Middle Ages 768–1487*, 1996
Kapelle, W.E., *The Norman Conquest of the North: the Region and its Transformation 1100–1135*, 1975
Lapper, I., and Parnell, G., *The Tower of London: a 2000-Year History*, 2000
Loyn, H.R., *The Norman Conquest*, 1965
Matthew, D., *The Norman Conquest*, 1966
Messent, J., *The Bayeux Tapestry Embroiderers' Story*, 1999
Morillo, S., *Warfare under the Anglo-Norman Kings 1066–1135*, 1994
Morillo, S., *The Battle of Hastings: Sources and Interpretations*, 1996
Morris, J., ed., *Domesday Book*, by county, various dates c.1980 on
Nicolle, D., *The Normans*, 1987
Scragg, D.G., ed., *The Battle of Maldon*, text, 1981
Scragg, D.G., ed., *The Battle of Maldon*, collected essays, 1991
Stenton, F.M., *Anglo-Saxon England*, 1971
Strickland, M., *Anglo-Norman Warfare*, 1992
Thorpe, L., *The Bayeux Tapestry and the Norman Invasion*, 1973
van Houts, E.M.C., ed., *The Gesta Normannorum Ducum of William of Jumièges, Orderic Vitalis, and Robert of Torigny*, 2 vols., 1994, 1998
Walker, I.W., *Harold, the Last Anglo-Saxon King*, 1997
Whitelock, D., *The Anglo-Saxon Chronicle*, 1961
Williams, A., *The English and the Norman Conquest*, 1995
Wilson, D.M., *The Bayeux Tapestry*, 1985
Wise, T., *Saxon, Viking and Norman*, 1979

Index

Figures in **bold** refer to illustrations or maps

Visit the Osprey website

- Information about forthcoming books

- Author information

- Read extracts and see sample pages

- Sign up for our free newsletters

- Competitions and prizes